Building Transitional Programs for Students with Disabilities

How to Navigate the Course of Their Lives

Christy Mahanay-Castro

ROWMAN & LITTLEFIELD EDUCATION

A division of

ROWMAN & LITTLEFIELD PUBLISHERS, INC.
Lanham • New York • Toronto • Plymouth, UK

Published by Rowman & Littlefield Education
A division of Rowman & Littlefield Publishers, Inc.
A wholly owned subsidiary of The Rowman & Littlefield Publishing Group, Inc.
4501 Forbes Boulevard, Suite 200, Lanham, Maryland 20706
http://www.rowmaneducation.com

Estover Road, Plymouth PL6 7PY, United Kingdom

British Library Cataloguing in Publication Information Available

Library of Congress Cataloging-in-Publication Data

Mahanay-Castro, Christy, 1963–
  Building transitional programs for students with disabilities : how to navigate the course of their lives / Christy Mahanay-Castro.
    p. cm.
  Includes bibliographical references.
  ISBN 978-1-60709-999-4 (cloth : alk. paper) — ISBN 978-1-61048-000-0 (pbk. : alk. paper) — ISBN 978-1-61048-001-7 (electronic)
    1. Students with disabilities—Education (Secondary)—United States. 2. Education, Secondary—Curricula—United States. 3. Special education—United States. I. Title.
  LC4031.M27 2010
  371.9'0473—dc22
                                                          2010028869

♾ ™ The paper used in this publication meets the minimum requirements of American National Standard for Information Sciences—Permanence of Paper for Printed Library Materials, ANSI/NISO Z39.48-1992.

Printed in the United States of America

Contents

Preface

This book is intended for high school special education teachers, school administrators, parents, and prospective special education teachers. It provides the perspective of high school graduates and the parents of those graduates who participated in a special education program for the majority of their public school education.

Throughout the book there are suggestions to special education and general education teachers and administrators to provide guidance and direction for building effective transition programs for high school students with disabilities. The last chapter of the book includes worksheets and activities for special education teachers to utilize with high school students with disabilities to supplement a transition curriculum for preparation into adult living.

Acknowledgments

I would like to thank my family, friends, and colleagues for their support during the writing of this book. I am especially grateful to Dr. Giovanna Parma for her contribution. I dedicate this book to my sons and students.

Chapter 1

An Introduction

It was the most unexpected place to have an epiphany regarding my life's work. I was getting my hair cut, and my hair dresser asked me what I did for a living. I replied that I was a special education teacher. The hair dresser said that her husband was enrolled in special education programs all throughout school and suffered poor self-esteem due to the labels put on him by the educators and his peers.

She told a story about how they went to a high school reunion 10 years after graduation, and one of his fellow classmates commented, "Oh, I remember you. You were in special ed!"

She proceeded to tell me about the damage inflicted on her husband a decade later, due to the school's special education program. She was appalled that a decade after her husband's graduation the prominent memory of his former classmate was still that of a label put upon him by the educational system.

There I was, sitting at the hair dresser's getting my hair cut, contemplating whether my life's work had done more harm than good. I not only taught special education, I had also spent several years as a director of special education. Had the career I lived over decades actually been causing devastation and destruction instead of helping students?

The words of my hair dresser stuck with me. Six years and many haircuts later, I had the opportunity to gain understanding of the perception of students with disabilities regarding their transition into adult living after high school graduation. I decided to research the subject by interviewing graduates from a special education program.

I chose to interview their parents as well. I wanted to get the perception of those who had been out of high school long enough to begin their lives, and

1

to be able to reflect on their education and how it did or did not benefit them in their transition into adult living.

I chose students who had graduated three to five years previous to my interviewing them, because I wanted them to have life experience to help them evaluate their preparation. I hoped to understand their perspective and make a contribution to my profession that would benefit general and special education administrators and teachers, special education teachers, students, and parents.

The focus of my research became: How did participation in special education help prepare students with disabilities for life beyond the public schools?

SPECIAL EDUCATION STORIES WERE
PART OF MY OWN LIFE

Over the past 25 years, I have held many positions in many different states in the public school system. I have been a special education teacher and a director of special education. I have been an assistant principal, a principal, and a teacher in alternative education as well as a general education classroom teacher.

During those 25 years, I have strived desperately to help students struggling with learning disabilities, as well as with an array of other disabilities, to improve their academic and social skills in order to be successful in the public school system, and to prepare them for their lives as adults.

I will begin by introducing some of the people who helped fuel my passion for this focus of research. Please keep in mind that I have changed the names of the people I have referred to in this book both from my life and those I interviewed in the research study to protect their privacy.

Mrs. Smith was a special education teacher who spent her career helping students with emotional disabilities. She spent many countless hours writing Individual Education Plans (IEPs) and involving herself in the academic, behavioral, and personal lives of her students. She passed away in 2003 of heart failure. Her students in Connecticut were devastated by their loss. Her dedication and contribution to her students was an inspiration to all.

Junior was a student in my high school alternative education class who had a learning disability and came from a dysfunctional family. The last words I heard from him before he passed away in a car wreck, were, "Mrs. Cortner, do you think I should go to summer school?"

I replied, "I think you've earned a break from school, Junior. Enjoy your summer!" That summer he and his friend were drinking and driving, and I never saw Junior again, because he did not survive the car wreck.

Nathan was a young man in my high school with a learning disability who had tremendous artistic talent. He, too, came from a dysfunctional family. He and I worked together with his art teacher to help him apply to a nearby art college.

He had his portfolio and application finished, and the only step left was to turn in the portfolio and application to the college. He had everything he needed including stamps. For unexplainable reasons, he chose not to complete the final step, and two years later he committed suicide.

David was another young man in one of my high school alternative education classes who was diagnosed with a learning disability. He had a hard time writing various English assignments, but he was able to write poetry with ease. He came in every morning to my class exhausted from working at a fast food restaurant the night before. He had a difficult childhood, but was getting ready to become a parent himself within several months.

He brought in the ultrasound of his unborn daughter with pride and fear to show me and his classmates. After sharing the picture, he sat down as usual to write poetry in his journal. The last words I heard him speak were, "Bye, Mrs. Cortner!" as he hung his body out of the car window, waving, and driving away from me.

He was on his way to a camping trip with his family that summer. The very next day he died heroically up in the mountains trying to save a couple stranded in the river in a canoe that was teetering on the edge of the waterfalls.

In one of the most tragic cases that I have ever experienced, I knew five young people Sally, Joe, Kevin, Jake, and Randy. Joe was a young man who was learning disabled. He came from a broken home and dropped out of high school. He joined the military and received an early discharge. Kevin was a graduate from high school and had been in the special education program for the majority of his education. Jake and Randy were at risk students who dropped out of school. Sally was the only one among the five friends who graduated from high school without being identified as a student with disabilities or low academic achievement.

All five of these young adults were friends and none of them had jobs. Sally and Kevin had a baby together who was hearing impaired. All five became involved in the local drug culture. One summer afternoon Sally and Kevin were murdered and their bodies thrown over an embankment, leaving their infant son without parents. The other three friends, Joe, Jake, and Randy were all charged with the murders. Joe and Randy were given life sentences for their role in the murders, and Randy also received a prison sentence for his role in the double homicide.

All of these young adults were friends, but their lack of direction and preparation for adult life contributed to their demise. Their involvement in the drug scene produced the dynamics in the group which caused mayhem in their lives and the lives of their families. Could the course of their lives have been changed by intervention and better transition planning?

These people in my life affected me and my beliefs regarding special education in various ways. The human frailty of these students and teachers enlightened me to the fact that the special education program can be a tremendous influence in the outcome of their lives. The transitional years of these students help them become productive citizens. What educators say and do with these students can be a determining factor in their lives.

PUBLIC SCHOOLS ARE REQUIRED TO PROVIDE TRANSITIONAL SERVICES FOR STUDENTS WITH DISABILITIES

Transitioning into adult living is difficult enough for students without disabilities. For students with disabilities it can be overwhelming. Most often their educational years are full of academic struggle that affects their self-confidence often to the point of giving up and dropping out. If they do not have job skills when they graduate, they can experience an extension of the struggle and lack of confidence they experienced in school.

All students, especially students with disabilities, need extensive vocational training; however many students do not receive the vocational training necessary to provide them with a solid foundation for transitioning into adult living.

I have seen high schools that had strong vocational programs where academics revolved around them. I believe that there should be more high school programs available like those.

In addition to vocational programs, students with disabilities also need an education that prepares them in other areas such as relationships, finances, employment, and parenting classes while they are still in high school.

It has been debatable in the past whether the public school system should be responsible for these programs. Because of the Individuals with Disabilities Education Act (IDEA), the federal law mandates that public schools provide transitional services for students with disabilities.

The 1990 Individuals with Disabilities Education Act (IDEA) addressed transition for students with disabilities. IDEA was revised in 1997 and again in 2004. It continued to stress the requirement for transitional services for students with disabilities. Therefore, it is the responsibility and legal obligation of our public schools to provide services that will facilitate successful transition.

SUCCESS FACTORS AND CHALLENGES

Many factors influence the success of students leaving secondary school special education programs. A student's way of thinking can be a positive or negative factor. If a student believes in him/herself and has a plan, goals and strategies, then these help to produce positive results. If a student has little or no self-confidence and no direction, he/she can become lost and flounder indefinitely.

Community partnership with the schools is a powerful factor, because these partnerships can provide work experience before the student leaves high school. Students who have work experience during their high school years have a greater chance of continuing employment.

Although the legislation was passed to assist students and educators in helping students with transition, unless the legislation is implemented properly, little progress can be made. There are vast challenges for students with disabilities to overcome in transitioning into adult living. The employment rate for students with disabilities is low.

The educational process has concentrated on the academic concerns of students with disabilities rather than preparing them for life after school. Students with disabilities have lower rates of employment, lower earnings, lower rates of postsecondary school attendance (and graduation), and lower rates of independent living status than do young adults without disabilities.

To compound the problem, if a student has emotional or behavioral problems, then they will probably lack impulse control and have difficulty managing their anger.

Poverty is a challenge which can prevent disabled students from transitioning successfully into postsecondary education and training programs. Absenteeism and high dropout rate can be correlated to students in poverty and students with disabilities. Students with disabilities that come from families of poverty are facing effects from both challenges. Dropping out of school and bad attendance habits can translate into low income jobs and poor work habits.

Graduates who find themselves unemployed, or in low income dead-end jobs, struggle with being independent. They will need to depend on others to survive. They often continue to live with parents or others because they cannot afford life's essentials.

They can find themselves needing government financial assistance. Some are unaware of the assistance that is available and are unable to independently apply for assistance because of low reading and writing abilities.

SUGGESTIONS FOR SPECIAL EDUCATION
TEACHERS AND STAFF

Many tragic human stories and situations can present themselves in the field of special education. Prospective special education teachers and staff should work in the field before pursuing this type of career. The work can take the form of paid or volunteer experience.

The field of special education can be emotionally and mentally demanding. It would benefit prospective teachers and staff to have previous experience before investing a great deal of their time and resources into such a career. Many people may not be prepared for these types of demands.

Teachers and staff who are in the special education field should have appropriate recreational outlets and hobbies to release emotional and mental tension that may be a result of the challenges and demands of the career.

Counseling may be needed and beneficial for teachers and staff to be able to continue in a field that has a high burnout rate. It is common for teachers and staff to take their job home with them and make it difficult to separate from their career, which may result in difficulties in their personal life.

SUMMARY

The federal law, Individuals with Disabilities Education Act, requires the public school system to provide transitional services for students with disabilities. The law evolved because of the vast unpreparedness of special education graduates for adult living.

Students with disabilities are presented with many challenges throughout their educational career. These challenges continue to affect them when transitioning into adult living. Most of these students do not continue on to higher education.

Therefore, a specialized program which involves addressing their challenges is necessary for their success. The many challenges that are faced by students with disabilities, such as poor self-esteem, unemployment, low wages, and dependent living all need to be addressed while they are still in high school.

Educators can affect the lives of students with mere words. The programs provided by school systems can be a catalyst to successful adult living for students with disabilities. Our schools have a tremendous journey ahead in order to accomplish the programming needed for successful transition.

Chapter 2

Laws Regarding Students with Disabilities

The Individuals with Disabilities Education Act mandates that every special education student (starting during the year the student turns 16 until graduation) have a transition plan. This chapter will review the evolution of special education law and the requirement of transition planning for students with disabilities.

Individual states were entitled to address the needs of students with disabilities as they saw fit until the enactment of federal law in 1975, which mandated that all states educate students with disabilities. It wasn't until 1990 that transition services were mandated to be addressed in the student individual education plans (IEPs).

1880–1950 INSTITUTIONALIZING THOSE WITH DISABILITIES AND MENTAL ILLNESS

In the late 1800s, there was an accepted and widespread practice in the United States to institutionalize the citizens who were considered mentally ill. In the early 1900s, handicapped children were excluded from school in most states. Some of these children were hidden behind closed doors and they never left home. Many of these handicapped children were institutionalized for life.

For the next 50 years, those with disabilities and mental illness were generally treated as outcasts. They were often thought of as being possessed by the devil. Sometimes they were institutionalized, and often they were left on the streets to fend for themselves. It was not uncommon for them to end up in prison.

7

1954–1970 INDIVIDUAL STATES HAD THE OPTION TO EDUCATE CHILDREN WITH DISABILITIES

Before the mid-1970s, it was up to the individual states to decide whether or not they would educate children with disabilities. There were millions of children with disabilities who did not attend school or did not receive help in the schools where they attended or were institutionalized.

Children were often refused admittance into the public schools or expelled due to their disabilities. It was not until the mid-1950s that the federal government became involved in passing laws affecting education.

Case law over the years has helped shape the progression of state and federal law and services for disabled children. *Brown vs. the Board of Education*, a United States Supreme Court case in 1954, ruled that *separate but equal education was not equal.*

This case not only ruled that racial segregation was unacceptable, it helped to shine light on the education of children with disabilities. It assisted in establishing the development of the concept of disabled students being educated among their nondisabled peers, by identifying all children, no matter their race, gender, or disability as being equal.

When the federal government passed the National Defense Education Act of 1958, which allocated grant money for math and science in the younger grades, it paved the way for the federal government to become more involved in public education. In 1965, the Elementary and Secondary Education Act (ESEA) was passed by the federal government to support special populations in school.

In 1966, more grants became available to help educate children with disabilities. Teacher training, research, and program models for disabled children were federally funded in the Johnson and Nixon administrations.

The two landmark federal court decisions, the 1972 *Mills v. Board of Education of the District of Columbia* and the 1971 decision of *Pennsylvania Association for Retarded Children v. Commonwealth of Pennsylvania*, established that educating students with disabilities is derived from the Fourteenth Amendment of the United States Constitution (Martin, 1996; Council for Exceptional Children, 2003).

1970–1989 FEDERAL LAW ADDRESSES CHILDREN WITH DISABILITIES

Students with learning disabilities were not specifically addressed in the law until the passing of the Education for All Handicapped Children Act of 1975. This law was the first law to include students with specific learning disabilities as a qualifying category for special education services.

This law helped students with a variety of disabilities qualify for special education services. However, they usually received a great deal of their education in the special education classroom away from their nondisabled peers, and without access to the general education curriculum.

In 1975, Public Law 94-142, Education for All Handicapped Children Act, was passed. It was initially introduced in 1969. It took six years for this law to get passed. This law mandated that all children with disabilities receive a free appropriate public education.

The Education for All Handicapped Children Act also promised to pay 40 percent of the extra cost that schools had to spend on educating students with disabilities. Unfortunately, to date the federal government has only paid up to approximately 15 percent of the total cost (Pardini, 2002).

The Education for All Handicapped Children Act of 1975 established Individual Education Plans (IEPs) and introduced the idea of students being educated in the Least Restrictive Environment (LRE).

Section 504 is a paragraph in The Rehabilitation Act of 1973, which was issued to begin with the 1977–78 school year. Section 504 is a protection for students with disabilities that prohibits discrimination and provides consequences of discontinuation of federal funding for districts which do not comply.

The Education of All Handicapped Children Act was amended in 1983 to include parent training and information centers, school to work transition programs, and early-intervention programs which were to be funded by each state.

The Education of All Handicapped Children Act was amended again in 1986 to include the award of reasonable attorneys' fees to parties who prevailed in court when suing school districts over issues regarding the education of children with disabilities.

In 1986, the Supreme Court ruled that special education students could also access rights and protections under Section 504 of The Rehabilitation Act of 1973. However, the reverse was not true. Those students who qualify for Section 504 protection do not necessarily qualify for special education services because the qualifications for special education services were usually more extensive and involved than for Section 504.

1990–2004 TRANSITION FOR STUDENTS WITH DISABILITIES ADDRESSED IN THE LAW

The 1990 Individuals with Disabilities Education Act (IDEA) addressed transition requirements and guidelines, as well as assistive technology. In addition, IDEA added qualifying categories for special education which included autism and traumatic brain injury. Services for infants and preschoolers were addressed again by amending Part H in 1992 of IDEA. States were mandated to ensure that all students receive a Free Appropriate Public Education (FAPE).

IDEA replaced Public Law 94-142. The transition services included all types of transition services. It included transition from preschool to kindergarten as well as transition from high school to adult living. Transition services evolved due to the need for students to transition successfully into kindergarten and into adult living after graduating from high school.

Parental rights were addressed and due process procedures were more clearly outlined in the 1990 reauthorization. Due process provided the parents with the legal option of disputing decisions and placements or other issues needing to be addressed by the school district and/or parents.

It also provided parents a guarantee of confidentiality regarding information in their child's school records. This prevented access to the child's records unless it was by school personnel for educational reasons.

In 1997, IDEA was reauthorized again, providing another opportunity to revise the law. Among the changes was the attempt to reduce paperwork for teachers and schools, but unfortunately, this was not realized. The reauthorization also put safeguards in place to prevent disproportionate special education identification of minorities.

During the 2000–2001 school year there were 2.9 million students with learning disabilities ages 3 to 21 being served in special education. This number had more than tripled since the 1976–77 school year (Schaeffer, 2005).

IDEA was reauthorized again in 2004. It was signed into law by President George W. Bush on December 3, 2004. There were many new amendments to IDEA in the 2004 reauthorization.

These major amendments included another attempt to reduce paperwork to provide more time for instructional purposes and improvement of the education for students with disabilities. Unfortunately, again, this has not been the reality in many school districts. Paperwork for special education was at an all time high and continued to be for future years following the 2004 reauthorization of IDEA.

Part B (Assistance for Education of All Children with Disabilities) of IDEA included many major amendments regarding state and local level activities. Behavioral supports were added. Disaggregation of suspension and expulsion rates by race and ethnicity was added.

State level maintenance of effort and state flexibility with funds, access to instructional material, disproportionate overidentification of students with disabilities by ethnicity, and the prohibiting of mandatory medication of students were among the many major changes to Part B of IDEA. Participation of all students in assessments, alternate assessments, and reports were also mandated.

Parental consent regarding evaluation and eligibility determination was changed. Parents were still allowed to initiate request for evaluation, but with the 2004 reauthorization, they were also allowed to decline consent for an initial evaluation for their child.

Assistive technology became something that must also be considered each year at the annual IEP. Assistive technology may be needed to help the student be successful in school and in other life activities such as communication. Assistive technology can be a variety of different devices such as a calculator, computer, software, and so on.

An exit summary was now to be provided for students exiting high school. The exit summary was intended to provide information regarding the student's disability and how the disability impacts his or her life activities.

The exit summary should help the student in his or her pursuit in obtaining adult services and indicate accommodations needed when attending postsecondary education and/or training and when obtaining a job. These are just a few of the many changes made by the 2004 reauthorization of IDEA.

The legislature is committed to reexamining IDEA regularly to provide the needed adjustments. As special education develops and the needs of special education students change, the law is adjusted to meet the needs of the students. These changes can be highly demanding on the school system, but are intended to be in the best interest of the students.

The Individuals with Disabilities Education Act Public Law 101-476 (IDEA) of 1990 was the first legislation to mandate that educators include a transition plan in the IEP for students transitioning out of high school and into adult life.

Although there has been legislation addressing transition planning for students with disabilities for more than a decade, students with disabilities continue to struggle with successful transition from public school into adult living. Unless schools make changes in the way they address this issue, there will continue to be problems with special education students transitioning into adult living.

In 1997, there was an effort to begin addressing transitional needs at 14 rather than 16, and even earlier if needed. In 2004 it was changed again to age 16. The transition plan should include several components. There should be measurable goals, activities, and a course of study.

Areas to be addressed include instruction, life skills, community and adult living, and vocational training. The plan is derived from a vocational evaluation, parent and student input, and input from all IEP members as well as any agency that may be involved in the transition planning.

Chapter 2

SUGGESTIONS FOR SPECIAL EDUCATION
TEACHERS AND STAFF

Special education teachers, administrators, and staff will need to know the special education federal law and state regulations. Special education is a litigious field and it is beneficial to staff, parents, and students when the law is well-known and understood.

It is easier to understand why a law is in existence when the evolution of the law is known. Knowing and understanding the special education law will help to make for a smoother process for everyone involved in the students' programs.

SUMMARY

The United States has come a long way regarding the education of children with disabilities. The early experiences for students with disabilities included institutionalization. They were often left to the streets to fend for themselves, and sometimes worked their way into jail and/or prison.

1880–1950 Institutionalizing those with disabilities and mental illness
1954–1970 Individual states had the option to educate children with disabilities
1954 Brown vs. the Board of Education
National Defense Education Act of 1958
1965, the Elementary and Secondary Education Act (ESEA) was passed
Mills v. Board of Education of the District of Columbia 1972
1971 decision of *Pennsylvania Association for Retarded Children v. Commonwealth of Pennsylvania*
Education for All Handicapped Children Act of 1975
Section 504 is a paragraph in The Rehabilitation Act of 1973
Education of All Handicapped Children Act was amended in 1983
The Education of All Handicapped Children Act was amended again in 1986
In 1986, the Supreme Court ruled that special education students could also access rights and protections under Section 504 of The Rehabilitation Act of 1973
The 1990 Individuals with Disabilities Education Act (IDEA) addressed transition
In 1997, IDEA was reauthorized
IDEA was reauthorized again in 2004

Figure 2.1. Special Education Timeline

In the 1950s the civil rights movement opened the eyes of the public to recognize that people with disabilities have a right to an equal education. The Education for All Handicapped Children Act of 1975 was the first federal law to address the education of students with disabilities.

The Education for All Handicapped Children Act was revised many times over the years to address (among many other issues) free appropriate public education, least restrictive environment, education for disabled preschool students, and transition services.

In 1997 and again in 2004 the Individuals with Disabilities Education Act was reauthorized. It will continue to be considered for reauthorization periodically to address the changing needs of students with disabilities.

Chapter 3

Special Education Services and the Individual Education Plan

This chapter will provide an overview of the continuum of special education services. The chapter will also outline the required elements of the IEP according to the 2004 reauthorization of IDEA including a brief overview of the transition component. Chapter 4 will present a more in-depth description of the transition plan.

SPECIAL EDUCATION DELIVERY OF SERVICES

Remedial instruction in special education helps to raise skills in academic areas. Students with disabilities can feel overwhelmed and lost in the general education classes. They may welcome the opportunity to be provided individualized and small group instruction in special education classes as well as additional support in the general education classrooms.

It is important to remember that isolation and grouping should be balanced. Students with disabilities should not be singled out as being different more than absolutely necessary. This is especially true once students reach secondary grade levels.

The process of identifying students with disabilities is determined by both federal law and state regulation. Each state defines what specific criteria must be met in order for a student to be identified with a disability. Federal law requires that this be a team process, preventing one single participant from unilaterally determining eligibility.

There are several special education delivery models that are practiced in the public school system. A continuum of services is best for the variety of special education needs in schools such as the inclusion model, the resource room model, and self-contained special education classroom. The service model chosen for each student should be a team-based decision. Each child is entitled by law to a free and appropriate public education in the least restrictive environment.

The inclusion model is a program model that maintains high expectations for all students. This is a program where general education classroom teachers and special education teachers and/or staff work together in the general education classroom to deliver education to all students.

The main goal of an inclusion model is for the students with disabilities to stay in the general education classroom for the entire day and receive special education services within the general education classroom. Remediation and accommodations can be made for all students who need it. All ranges of disabilities can be included in this model with the appropriate staff support.

The resource room is a special education instructional model which pulls students with disabilities out of the general education classroom and into a separate classroom for specialized instruction for a portion of the day. The resource room can be helpful due to the efforts of individual teachers who provide remediation, individual assistance, and positive reinforcement.

When this occurs, then the schools risk publicly identifying those students as being different from their peers, and can possibly cause self-esteem and self-image issues for students with disabilities.

Resource classrooms should not put students with mild disabilities into a separate class with students with severe cognitive delays. This practice can further damage the self-esteem and self-image of the students with mild disabilities.

There is a chance that students with mild delays and their peers could identify them as having more severe disabilities. Nonetheless, the resource room can be helpful due to the efforts of the individual teachers who provide remediation, individual assistance, research-based curriculum, and positive reinforcements.

The self-contained model provides instruction for students with disabilities in a special education classroom for the majority of the day. Most often students with severe cognitive disabilities and students with severe behavioral disabilities are placed in a self-contained delivery model.

The self-contained model is typically considered the most restrictive environment. However, this program model may be the best placement for some students. If the student is able to gain the most progress in this type of restrictive environment, then it can be the correct placement for him/ or her.

INDIVIDUAL EDUCATION PLAN

An Individual Education Plan (IEP) is required by the Individuals with Disabilities Education Act (IDEA) to take place each year for students with disabilities. According to the law, an IEP is "comprehensive, specific, sequential, realistic and appropriate, understandable, and mutually developed." According to the federal law, IDEA, there are certain required components of an IEP.

These include a group of "required team members, a statement of a student's present level of performance in areas of concern, related services, the least restrictive environment, an explanation of the student's participation in state and district testing, the special education service time and location, goals, transition services (if age appropriate), assistive technology, progress, accommodations, and general education progress."

REQUIRED COMPONENTS OF AN IEP

Required Team Members

The IEP is ongoing and flexible. It is a student-based plan that includes the student's strengths, interests, preferences, needs, and skills. The process of developing the IEP is a shared responsibility of a group of people who know and work with the student. A complete team must meet in order for the IEP to be an official document.

The required core participants of an IEP team include the parent(s), special education teacher, a general education teacher, and an administrator. Additional members may include the student, additional school personnel, and other local agency representatives that are necessary, as well as anyone else that the parent of the student with disabilities would like to invite.

If any of these members are absent from an IEP meeting, then the parent must give written permission excusing them. The absent member can give their input in writing to be reviewed at the IEP meeting.

Present Level of Performance

The student's current level of performance is measured by observations, classroom tests, evaluations, and input by the IEP team members. When writing the present level of performance, it is important to keep in mind the reader's perspective.

The reader should be able to identify appropriate goals from the information given in the present level of performance statement. It should address the student's strengths, areas of need, and include how the student's disability will affect his/her performance in the general education classroom. The present level of performance should be written objectively and measurably.

Related Services

Related services are support services such as counseling, speech therapy, occupational, and physical therapy. Transportation is also considered a related service. If the student needs the school district to provide transportation in order for the student to access his or her education, then transportation must be provided.

Least Restrictive Environment

The least restrictive environment addresses participation with nondisabled students. It includes the amount of time a student will participate in the general education classroom, curriculum, and other nonacademic school-related activities.

Participation in Testing

Participation in district, state, and classroom testing must be clearly documented on the IEP. Accommodations for tests must be indicated. The district and state test accommodations must be directly related to the accommodations made in the classroom. If a test is not appropriate for the student, then the team must explain why and establish eligibility for alternative testing.

Service Time and Location

Statement of when and where the special education services are to occur allows the parents to know exactly how much time their child is spending in special education, and how much time, if any, they are absent from their general education classroom. It also explains how often the service will be provided, the length of time for each service, and the service provider. The goals should be tied to each service on the IEP.

Goals

Academic, behavioral, and transition goals (when age appropriate) are required on IEPs for areas of service. These are annual and measurable goals that can be reasonably reached by the child. The goals are to be broken down into objectives if the student is taking an alternative assessment rather than the required state testing.

Assistive Technology

Assistive technology is equipment or an assistive device that facilitates the student in being successful in school and life. The assistive technology can be as basic as pictures facilitating communication, or as high tech as a computer.

Progress

Parents must be informed at least quarterly about the progress their child is making on the IEP goals. How progress toward the goals will be measured and delivered as well as when the progress will be reported to the parents must be explained on the IEP.

Accommodations

Accommodations and modifications are sometimes necessary in order for the student to access the general education curriculum. Accommodations are adjustments made to the environment or assignments and/or the instruction to assist in accessing the curriculum. If modifications are made, then there is an alteration of the curriculum.

Accommodations are more commonly made for students than modifications are. It may be necessary for students to receive accommodations or modifications for testing, assignments, instruction, and/or to the school environment and/or curriculum.

General Education Curriculum Participation

Students in special education are expected to make progress in the general education curriculum. The IEP team should be aware of the general education standards at the student's grade level and those standards that apply to the student's IEP goals. Academic goals will usually be on a lower level than the student's grade level standards. The IEP goals should serve as sequential steps that lead to the eventual attainment of the grade level standards.

TRANSITION PLAN

The Individuals with Disabilities Education Act requires that the IEP contains a transitional plan the year a student turns 16 years old and every year thereafter (or younger if the IEP team determines it is necessary). There are many required components of the transition plan. The transition plan should be approached by taking a realistic look at what the student's skills and interests are.

A vocational assessment and/or inventory is required to be conducted to help assess possible vocational skills and interests. The student must be invited to the meeting to participate in the IEP.

The parents' and student's opinions and desires should be a focal point in the process. In order for the transition plan to be effective, the school must have an appropriate vocational and life skills program.

The plan should be outcome based, which emphasizes activities that promote school to post-school activities, and include postsecondary education, vocational training, integrated employment, supported employment, adult education, adult services, independent living, and/or community participation.

There is a requirement in the IEP for a statement regarding the transfer of rights at least one year before the age of majority (18) is reached. There should also be measurable postsecondary goals, activities, and a course of study. Student invitation and participation should be documented.

The transition plan is derived from vocational assessments, parent and student input, and input from all IEP team members as well as any agency that may be involved in the transition planning. The transition services and activities to be reviewed and included are instructional needs, related services, community experience, employment needs, post-school adult living goals, general education instruction, special education instruction, support, and related services.

SUGGESTIONS FOR SPECIAL EDUCATION TEACHERS AND STAFF

Paperwork is a large part of being a special education teacher. Therefore being prepared and organized is an essential skill for this career. Strict federal and state timelines for special education paperwork determine the amount of paperwork due at any given time.

The law changes periodically which can dictate a change in the required paperwork involved in special education programs. Keeping up with the paperwork requirements can be stressful and overwhelming.

It is helpful to have an organized list of students and what paperwork is required throughout the year and the dates they are due. If this list is completed at the beginning of the year and updated throughout the year, then the special education teacher will know what paperwork is due each month, and it may help the teacher to meet the critical deadlines for the required paperwork.

Administrators should promote substitute time so special education teachers can prepare paperwork.

SUMMARY

The Individual Education Plan (IEP) has many required components. It must contain a statement of the student's present level of performance in the student's areas of need. It must have measurable goals, how and when progress on the goals are measured and delivered.

Related services, accommodations, assessment accommodations, and a transition plan if the student is going to turn age 16 during the year of the IEP (or sooner if the IEP team deems necessary) are also part of the IEP.

The transition plan must include certain requirements as well. There must be postsecondary measurable goals, a course of study, and activities needed for students to reach the goals. It must also contain a statement regarding the clarification of the transfer of rights. For the IEP which includes the transition plan, the student must be invited and his or her participation should be encouraged by the age of 16 and every IEP thereafter.

Chapter 4

The Transition Plan

The transition plan is included in the Individual Education Plan (IEP) starting the year that the student turns 16 years old (or younger if the IEP team deems it necessary), and every year thereafter until the student graduates from high school. The transition plan has many required components.

The transition plan includes student invitation to meetings, measurable postsecondary goals based on a vocational assessment, a course of study and activities necessary for the student to reach the post secondary goals.

The activities must address areas of instruction, life skills (if appropriate), community and adult living, related services, and vocational education and/ or training. It must also contain a statement regarding the clarification of the transfer of rights from parents to students.

Student Invitation and Participation

In general it is a good idea to invite the student to his or her IEP meetings from the time the student is able to understand and assist in the development of the program plan. According to IDEA, inviting the student to the IEP with transition services is no longer an option, but a requirement.

Documentation of the invitation of students to their transition planning should be made on the meeting invitation sent out for the IEP. It does not stop at student invitation however. Students are to be encouraged to participate in the transition plan. This chapter explores the student-centered or student-directed approach to facilitate student participation and to maintain focus on the student.

A student-centered or-directed IEP and transition plan is an outcome-based process which involves the student. It is especially important that students participate in the development of the transition portion of their IEP. The parents and professionals on the team should be aware of what they say about the student and how they say it. They should be supportive of the student and make it a positive experience.

It is important that students do not get the wrong idea about their abilities during this process. It is all too easy to stress the student's weaknesses rather than the student's strengths. If this is the case, the student may feel poorly about him or herself.

On the contrary, the student should leave the meeting feeling positive about his or her abilities. Therefore, emphasize the student's strengths and interests. The team members should think from the perspective of the student and conduct the meeting in a manner that they feel would be productive for the student.

There is a delicate balance which should be maintained in the student participation process. On one hand, the team should emphasize the student's strengths and ensure a positive outcome. However, the student should not gain a false sense of ability.

The student should know where he or she needs support and remediation. A true reflection of his or her achievement level should be presented. This balancing act is important and takes skill on behalf of the adult members of the team. Teachers and parents should be prepared to support students with sensitive issues.

The student should also have an understanding of what his or her disability is, what it means, and how it affects the student's learning process and style. The other team members in the process must also feel comfortable with having the student involved. There should be time for the students to develop skills related to IEP participation on a regular basis.

Students should have preparation and support when they participate in the IEP process. Some students can direct their own meeting, or they can direct parts of their meeting. Skills they need in order to participate actively in their own IEP include knowing how to choose goals based on their skills, interests, and limitations.

Students need to develop self-determination and self-advocacy skills. They also need to be taught how to accomplish goals. They need to learn how to devise a plan to attain their goals by making an action plan, and being able to adjust their plan of action when needed.

Self-determination skills can begin as early as in the elementary grades. Students need to be taught what an IEP actually is and the purpose of it. Any

Figure 4.1.   Student Centered Planning

questions regarding the IEP process should be addressed between the student and teacher.

It is possible to teach a course on participating in their IEP. Motivational techniques, such as having guest speakers who are successful even though they have a disability, may help students become interested in the IEP process as well as help them realize their own potential. Teachers must also communicate with the families and let them know the importance of their child's participation in their own IEP.

Figure 4.1 is a diagram representing a student-centered IEP and transition plan. The diagram puts the student in the center, with the team members and topics directed toward the student.

VOCATIONAL ASSESSMENT

A vocational assessment is the gathering of information regarding the student's abilities and interests in assisting the student in directions toward suitable vocations. The process includes inventories, surveys, observations, tests, work experience (both paid and volunteer), and subjective data.

Formal vocational assessments are available to assist in the process. The vocational assessment should be purposeful and well designed and take place over a period of time. Using a vocational assessment to identify areas of interest, strengths, and needs will provide a foundation for the student-based planning.

Finding the "best fit" for students with disabilities and employment is a productive form of planning for students with disabilities. Not only must strengths and weaknesses be considered, along with talents and interests, but the employers themselves, and their tolerance of "disabilities," is an essential component of finding a good fit.

Some employers are more tolerant and willing to train employees in areas where they need more assistance. There have been many famous and successful people in history with learning disabilities. These people were successful in finding a good fit between their skills, strengths, and interests, and occupations.

The IEP team will generate possibilities for the student to explore based on the vocational assessment. If the student has a variety of work experiences it could help in determining which vocation is the best fit for him or her.

The assessment should be adjusted over time as new information develops. Students can also volunteer in the community and conduct interviews with different professionals in order to better understand the jobs and careers available in the community.

POSTSECONDARY GOALS

Many factors influence the success of students leaving secondary school special education programs. A student's way of thinking, which includes a plan, goals, and strategy can be a positive factor. Goal setting is a major part of the IEP and the transition plan. Simply identifying areas of interest is not enough. The postsecondary goals should be reasonably attainable as well as measurable.

All too often the goals and objectives are generated and written by the special education teacher. Then the teacher presents the goals to the IEP team for their approval. Although the intention behind goal setting is to do it as a team, with the student being a big part of the decision, too often it is not done as it was intended.

Goals are set in life in order to obtain something. The student is the one who should be participating in communicating to the IEP team what the student wishes to accomplish or obtain in his or her life.

The student should be asked at least annually to generate transitional goals for the IEP meeting. The student should be thinking about and working toward his or her future goals throughout the year. If the goals are internalized by the student, there is a greater chance of effectiveness. Ambition is a productive trait which can result from students setting and reaching their goals.

Goal setting is important for all people in a variety of areas such as academics, top-level athletes, businesses, and other fields. It provides motivation and recognition when done properly. Self-motivation can be accomplished by students setting goals to reach their desired achievement and seeing their own progress toward that end.

One of the difficulties in IEP and transition goal setting is the student taking ownership over the goals and the goals being converted into intrinsic motivation for the student. Goals should be written based on the student's desires, beliefs, skills, and values. Internalizing the goals will help build motivation toward accomplishing the goals. The goals need to be reviewed at least annually.

Motivation can be lost if students are unwilling to make adjustments when their circumstances change. Students need to be willing to redefine their goals when necessary in order to stay on the path of success.

If a student finds the work or level of work too difficult, then the time frame may need to be extended, or other adjustments may need to be made. Personal circumstances need to be taken into consideration as well, so that adjustments can be made when necessary.

Self-determination is a characteristic that evolves in a student and is needed to succeed in adult life. Through the development of intrinsic goals, desires, values, and beliefs, self-determination is more likely to evolve. A student must be in control of his or her own destiny, and be made aware, and believe that he or she is capable of doing just that.

COURSE OF STUDY

The course of study is a list of educational classes the student will be taking in high school in order to graduate. The course of study is generated by the IEP team. The course of study that is standard for all general education students is available from the school counselor.

The general education course of study should be used to guide the team through the process. The school district where the student is attending school has graduation requirements based on certain mandatory courses and a predetermined number of credits. The IEP team should review this required course of study and apply what is relevant to the student.

If there are elective courses such as vocational classes, job experience, life skill classes, and so on that would better prepare the student for adult living, then the team can indicate the changes in the course of study.

ASSESSMENTS

The state and district assessments that the student is required to take in order to graduate must also be indicated. If a student will be expected to take the same state and district assessments as students without disabilities, then the IEP must indicate this. If the student is expected to take an alternative assessment or an alternate route to graduation, then the team must provide the plan for doing so.

DIPLOMA OR ALTERNATE CERTIFICATES

Some school districts offer something called a certificate of completion rather than a high school diploma. If this is the plan for a student on an IEP, then the future repercussions should be explored. For instance, some vocational training programs and colleges may not accept students who have a certificate of completion rather than the standard high school diploma typically received by most graduates.

ACTIVITIES NECESSARY FOR THE STUDENT TO REACH POST SECONDARY GOALS

The transition element of the IEP requires the team to explain various activities for the student to participate in. The types of activities include instruction, education and training, community involvement, and adult agencies.

Instruction

Instruction in the transition plan refers to content and delivery. Instruction should be delivered with accommodations that are necessary for the student to benefit. Method of delivery should be according to how the student learns best.

If the student is a strong auditory learner, then instruction of new concepts should be delivered verbally. If the student is a strong visual learner, then there should be visual aids in the delivery of instruction. Many students learn best when the instruction is applicable to the student's life, and/or when there are hands-on activities involved.

Instruction for transition includes a variety of classes which the IEP team believes is necessary for the student to succeed in adult living. There may be additional academic classes needed such as remedial reading or remedial math. Economics, health class, and other classes should be considered based on the student's strengths and areas of need.

Preparation for Postsecondary Education/Training

Programs should provide the academic support to assist students with disabilities to follow the path of post secondary education in addition to vocational training. Students who demonstrate a desire to go to college or other postsecondary training should be involved in a curriculum which prepares the student with disabilities to accomplish this goal.

The most difficult transition would be for a student with learning disabilities to attend a four-year college or a university. This is because students in high school have more teacher contact time, whereas in college the teacher contact time is less, and the student-to-teacher ratio is much higher.

In addition, the students' time is more structured in high school, with parental, teacher, and other staff support. In high school there is more frequent testing over the content area and students usually have more assistance with test taking.

In college, there is less structure, less support, and many of the college classes only test twice, once during midterms, and the final exam. This type of testing can be overwhelming for the student without disabilities, and very much so for the student with disabilities.

For a student with disabilities who intends on attending college after graduating from high school, the educational plan should include college preparation courses. Although often times the student may be encouraged to take easier classes in order to obtain a higher grade point average, the better decision might be to direct the student to take the college preparation courses with adequate support.

Some school districts have a partnership with the local community college and students can take dual credit classes. These classes give students college credit as well as high school credit. Students with disabilities desiring the college-bound path would best be suited to take more of these classes offered by the high school and the college.

If these classes are attended by students with disabilities, the college instructor should be aware of the students' disabilities and needed accommodations. Necessary remedial support must be provided for students who are on the college-bound path. Study skills should be taught in order to assist the student with the strenuous academic load.

If the student takes community college classes during his or her high school years and is successful, then the chances of success when transitioning into college, especially continuation in the local community college, will be increased. It is crucial that the student who wishes to attend college learn about his or her disability and how it affects learning.

Colleges do not always allow the same types of accommodations and/or modifications that high school allows. Therefore, it is important to review the accommodations and modifications on the IEP to determine which will still apply once the student is enrolled in college. Self-advocacy is also an important skill that a college-bound student must learn.

These students should visit the college(s) they plan to attend during their junior and senior years of high school. The students should make contact with the counselors at the college and be made aware of the tutoring programs and other resources available to students at the college under the Section 504 Rehabilitation Act of 1973.

The student should visit the office on campus that assists students with disabilities. Section 504 mandates that colleges provide equal opportunity for students with disabilities while the quality of education remains the same.

Vocational Programs

The goal of the vocational classes is to help the students develop an awareness, appreciation, and exploration of the various careers. It is crucial that students in special education receive an academic education. Each student should be able to read, write, and do math to the best of his or her capabilities. However, only 4 percent of students in special education ever enroll in a four-year college within three to five years after high school (Levine & Wagner, 2005).

This does not mean that schools should focus only on vocational programs, but that this reality should be taken seriously, and high schools should provide a vocational program.

This type of programming will allow for graduates to apply to community colleges, trade schools, and employment after graduation, instead of the statistical probability of being unprepared for postsecondary education or training and/or employment.

Independent Living

The life skills, parenting, and teen living classes are those that help students learn about life at home, social and personal relationships, and parenting skills. These classes often have a state curriculum that covers many subjects.

These subjects may include exploratory family and consumer science, young living, technology, life and careers, teen living, nutrition and foods, parenting and child development, career and personal development, personal and family finance and economics, adult living, family health and wellness, teen parenting, health care and human services occupations, and food science and nutrition.

If the school board agrees, then sex education can be included in either this program or a health class. Due to the fact that teaching sex education is controversial, it is usually not addressed to the extent needed by students with disabilities.

"Teens with disabilities often do not receive information on sexuality and reproductive health because parents or professionals either are unaware that teens with disabilities engage in sexual activity or are unable to discuss sensitive issues and acknowledge sexuality" (Seiler, 2001).

A basic level of consumer finance should be in place to help students with personal finance such as paying bills, living expenses, banking, rent, and so on. Classes should include low income housing requirements.

Community Participation

In order to transition into adult living students should participate in community activities. Often students already do this with their families or independently. The transition portion of the IEP requires special students to participate in community activities.

If the student cannot identify community participation, then the IEP team should generate activities in which the school can facilitate participation. Examples of community participation activities are going to the library, museums, movies, restaurants, the post office, and other places in the community.

Joining community groups such as Boy Scouts, a bowling team, and other community groups can be encouraged. Church group activities and other organizations can be listed as community activities.

ADULT SERVICES

Services for adults such as Supplemental Security Income, vocational rehabilitation, mental health services, health insurance, welfare, and other services
are to be included in consideration for the student's transition plan. A student
may need coordination of counseling services such as drug and alcohol and
mental health services as part of the transition plan.

Adult services may include sheltered working and living. It may be a group
home or perhaps it can take the form of semi-independent working and living
where an agency assists the student in the work and home environments.

It is required to have the student and/or family sign a release or exchange of
information form before sending confidential information to the agencies or
service providers. If a provider or agency requests information, and a release
has been signed, then it is important to be prompt in sharing the requested
information.

AGENCIES

Students with disabilities may qualify for services from private and state
agencies. Some of these services may be service coordination, intense behavioral intervention, counseling, and/or psychological services. If the student
needs outside services, it is necessary to invite these service providers to the
student's transition planning.

With the student's and parents' written permission, these service agencies
need to be part of the planning. Inviting outside agencies is important to the
educational planning, but if the teacher fails to get permission to invite, then
they are violating the confidentiality laws.

The student and parents need to be aware of what services will continue
after graduation and which services will be terminated. Vocational rehabilitation services may be part of the transitional plan for some students.

Inviting the agencies for adult services allows the student to be aware that
these adult services are available. It introduces a dialogue between the student
and his or her family and the agencies.

The high school, or more specifically, the special education teacher and/or
counselor in the high school, can help facilitate ongoing dialogue between the
student and agencies. The needs of the student and the agencies available for
support can be matched together to assist in the student's transition.

It is time during the transition planning to establish a shared responsibility between the school, community, and outside agencies for adult services.
In order to accomplish this type of shared responsibility, the schools need to

establish a good working relationship with these agencies. Inviting the agencies in advance, and giving them ample notice if a meeting is canceled, will go a long way in building a good working relationship with them.

RELATED SERVICES

Related services are required for the IEP and for the transition portion of the IEP as it applies to the transition plan. Related services may include transportation to get the student to and from community experiences, vocational training, job shadowing, and other transition activities.

Related services may refer to any support services needed by the student to transition into adult living such as counseling, speech therapy, physical therapy, occupational therapy, social services, nursing needs, and psychological services. Related services in the transition plan will concentrate on the services necessary for transitional needs rather than just the student's academic needs.

TRANSFER OF RIGHTS

Parents of children in special education are entitled to certain rights on behalf of their child under the Individuals with Disabilities Education Act. These rights transfer to the student once the student turns age 18. The law requires that there is a statement of explanation in the transition plan when the student is 17 years old explaining that these rights are transferred to the student once they turn 18, unless otherwise determined.

EXIT SUMMARY

An exit summary is a document or collection of documents that identify the student's disability and need for continuing accommodations if necessary. The document can be a collection of the latest IEP and eligibility report.

It can be a report written by the special education teacher and/or school psychologist that summarizes the student's area of disability. It should include the impact of the disability on the student's life and how it will affect the student when transitioning into adult living. The student should be able to use the exit summary to assist in applying for adult services and postsecondary education and/or training.

SUGGESTIONS FOR SPECIAL EDUCATION
TEACHERS AND STAFF

When conducting an IEP meeting the special education teacher or case manager should have an agenda. The first few items on the agenda should include the student's name and grade, the date and time the meeting starts and the time it is expected to finish.

The time limit to the average IEP should be approximately 30 minutes to an hour. Be careful of meeting longer than one hour because when a meeting goes too long it can become unproductive. Team members can become tired and confrontational.

Be sure to include introductions at the beginning of the meeting agenda. Always be sure to address the student's accomplishments and strengths at the beginning of the meeting to start the meeting on a positive note. When the agenda has the student's strengths and accomplishments listed at the beginning, then the team will remember to address this first.

The last agenda item should be a question regarding the date and time of the follow-up IEP meeting if necessary. When this item is on the agenda it prevents team members from believing they must address every issue at the meeting, thus allowing for ideas to be introduced and discussed, but preventing marathon meetings.

Adhering to an agenda keeps the team on task and can prevent unstructured and confrontational discussions. It allows for turn taking and time for each team member to be heard. Do not forget to put time on the agenda for student and parent input.

SUMMARY

The transition plan is a required part of the IEP during the year the student turns 16 years of age and every year thereafter. The transition plan includes the following components: invitation of the student, post secondary goals, a course of study, and activities necessary for the student to reach the post secondary goals.

Other areas to be addressed include instruction, life skills, community and adult living, related services, and vocational training. A vocational assessment needs to be conducted to assist in the planning. Also, notification of the transfer of rights from parents to students is required at the age of 17.

Student involvement in the creating of the transition plan is one of the most important aspects of the transition plan. The student's ownership of the plan can determine whether or not it is successful.

It is from the educational setting and school environment and into adult living that these students are transitioning. Therefore it is essential that they realize their adult role within the community, the world of work and independent living. The ability for students to access the needed adult services can be a determining factor in the student's success and quality of life.

Chapter 5

Parent Involvement and the Family

"There is no doubt that it is around the family and the home that all the greatest virtues, the most dominating virtues of human society, are created, strengthened and maintained."

Winston Churchill

It is parent participation that ensures that teachers understand the child's strengths and limitations. Parents must express to the team through IEP meetings and transition meetings the goals they would like to see their child accomplish. It is often through the guidance and dedication of parents that a child is able to live independently and to obtain employment and community resources.

An IEP meeting that is conducted appropriately can help with communication and prevent misunderstandings and conflicts. Parents can feel extremely intimidated at these meetings, so it is important that the meeting begin with introductions, and a presentation of the student's strengths. Making the student and parent feel comfortable and welcome in these meetings is important for an effective special education IEP meeting and program.

Often times these meetings can be viewed by the parents as a time when they and their child are being attacked and they may feel the need to be defensive. If a parent is feeling defensive then it is far more difficult for productive educational planning to take place. There are times when conflict is unavoidable, so teachers and school administrators should help to create an environment where conflict can be channeled into productive problem solving.

Parents can locate and access advocacy groups and state mediators by contacting the state department of education to assist when there are conflicts and to facilitate effective communication. Schools do not always welcome advocacy groups because the group or agency may facilitate more conflict between the parents and schools.

This is not always the case however. Advocacy groups may be able to assist in locating resources for the child's educational and transition needs as well as provide an objective perspective.

Many parents and/or guardians lack involvement in the education of their child. They may be busy with work, family illness, domestic violence, and other matters which can take priority. However, parents that get involved with their child's education can see positive results.

There are many ways for parents to guide and support their child's transition. Parents can become more aware of their child's learning strengths and needs, and communicate them to the IEP team to build the best program for their child.

Parents should be encouraged to inform the school of how and what they envision for their child's education and future. The IEP members should value the opinions of parents and work to implement their wishes when it is in the best interest of the student.

What is best for the student should be the focus of discussion, not what is best for the school, teachers, or parents. If there is a conflict in opinion, then it is the responsibility of the team to view the situation or problem through the eyes of the parents and student and to help the parents and student understand the school's perspective to work toward a consensus.

It may be believed that parents instinctively know how to get involved in their child's education, but this may not always be the case. It is important that schools take a role in helping parents become more involved. Teachers may need training and professional development to learn to work with families and to help them get more involved in their child's education.

To get optimum benefit, there should be family, school, and community involvement. The school, community, and family need to work together to provide positive outcomes for their children, and to help them become employable adults in the community.

A transition questionnaire for parents and students can be a helpful tool for IEP meetings and transition planning. The questionnaire should be given to the parents and students before the IEP in order to give them time to think about their input. The IEP team should review the questionnaires together and work to implement their ideas into the planning for the student where and when appropriate.

Parents can also help their child explore career interests and aptitudes through coordinating visits and tours to businesses and schools. They can encourage their child to volunteer and/or obtain part-time work. Parents can also learn to be consistent, patient, and persistent when necessary.

FAMILY

Family problems such as abuse, family illness, teen parents, and neglect are among the challenges that students with disabilities may have to cope with. A large percent of youth with disabilities come from low income households.

Family structure is a concern for students with disabilities since many of them come from homes with only one parent and many have parents who have not completed high school. If possible, schools should offer parenting classes and coordinate to provide these classes with outside agencies for parents and for high school students.

It may be necessary for families to obtain outside counseling to develop coping strategies for the family and for the child with disabilities. Counseling can help the family understand their child's behavior and way of thinking. The family should persist in developing an understanding of their child and his/her disability.

Children with disabilities may find themselves frustrated because they cannot do things as easily and quickly as their nondisabled siblings. This may cause low self-esteem issues. Sometimes siblings may find themselves being over protective, or even embarrassed by their disabled siblings. Nondisabled siblings may find themselves having to play a surrogate parental role because of the high demands of a sibling with disabilities.

Children with disabilities may believe what others say about them, even if it is thoughtless and careless, like saying they are "slow" or "different." Often times these children have a difficult time making friends. They usually demand more of their parents' time and energy, and this may cause jealousy among the siblings. The parents and other family members may experience an array of feelings including resentment, blame, and guilt.

Many emotions and behaviors such as aggressiveness can present a problem for children with disabilities. Aggression and anger in childhood may result in long-term unemployment in adulthood. Aggression modeled in the family environment can also be a factor that influences children to be aggressive in childhood and increase unemployment during adulthood.

Child-centered parenting (supportive parents, parents involved in their children's lives, and a warm family environment) and positive social behavior (high self-control of emotions in stressful or uncomfortable situations) can reduce aggressive children's chances of long-term unemployment.

Behavioral problems in school do not magically disappear after graduation from high school. It is not uncommon for students with behavioral problems to get involved in the legal system and experience problems with drugs and alcohol.

Schools can collaborate with parents and the community mental health and counseling providers, as well as agencies and groups to coordinate services that can carry over into life after high school. All collaboration with outside agencies must be done with parental permission (or student permission if the student is age 18 or older).

When children are maladjusted in school, there is less chance that as an adult, they will go on to higher education and employment. However, if a parent exhibits greater interest and involvement in school, it can positively affect a child's school performance. Parent involvement can monitor and change the outcome of a child's success in school and life.

Parents can be involved in their child's education through volunteering in the classroom, and after-school activities. Communicating with the child at home and actively participating in the child's life in the home and community environment is as important as helping them at school.

As children get older parents must provide guidance and assistance, and reinforce autonomy. Parents must talk to their children about making good choices on a daily basis. When parents are involved in their children's lives as a whole then they become more of an influence in their lives.

SUGGESTIONS FOR SPECIAL EDUCATION TEACHERS AND STAFF

School districts are financially responsible for services and placements recommended by the IEP team for students with disabilities. Before recommending counseling or other services for students it is critical to talk with and invite to the IEP meeting the school administrator responsible for committing funds.

Teachers and administrators can facilitate a welcoming environment in IEP meetings by providing a standard agenda which indicates a starting and ending time, introductions and the student's strengths. School staff should use respectful language and avoid inappropriate humor at the child's expense.

When schools provide a meal with a school activity, then there is usually a higher rate of attendance. "Dinner and a Book" is an activity where parents are invited to the school for a low-cost dinner and the parents sit with their child and read a book to them. There are a variety of creative ways to encourage parents to visit the school and food seems to be a great enticer.

SUMMARY

Parent involvement is an important part of successful transition of students with disabilities into adult living. This component may be easily overlooked by both schools and parents. Schools have the obligation of encouraging parents to participate in their child's educational program. Creating a welcoming environment at IEP meetings where transition is being discussed is a start.

Parents are usually very active with their child's education when their child begins school in preschool and kindergarten. There is a tendency to become less involved as the child progresses through their education into high school.

Parents must be concerned and actively participate with their older children at home. They need to guide them through the tumultuous teenage years and into adult living. It is at this point in their lives that they may need their parents the most.

Helping their children develop autonomy begins at a young age and continues throughout their early adult years. Various organizations and community resources are available for assistance. Parent advocacy groups may be a resource for parents and students. Churches, colleges, and social agencies may also provide resources and guidance.

Partnership with the school, parents, and community agencies is exactly what the transition process is about. Bringing together parents, community agencies, and the student to work together to develop a future beyond secondary education is a team process. Working as a team is the key to a successful transition.

Chapter 6

Experiences after High School Graduation

"Character cannot be developed in ease and quiet. Only through experience of trial and suffering can the soul be strengthened, ambition inspired, and success achieved."

Helen Keller

What are special education students doing after high school graduation? Figure 6.1 is a chart of research participants (students with disabilities), who were interviewed three to five years after graduation from high school. The interviews in this research were conducted in 2005 and 2006.

The chart provides their basic demographics including their area of disability, age, graduation year, and their living and employment situation after graduation. The names of all participants have been changed to protect their identity. This chapter is an informative reflection of research gathered through interviews with these students and their parents.

EMPLOYMENT EXPERIENCES OF SPECIAL EDUCATION GRADUATES

John

John lived with his grandparents off and on through school since his parents were truck drivers and were out of town a great deal. His grandmother, Grace, was a woman in her early seventies. She and John were from a close Christian family and went to church regularly with spirituality as a major family emphasis. John's parents were working and living in Nevada at the time of the interview.

Pseudonym Of Graduates	Disability	Age	Year of Graduation	Independent Living	Employment	Hourly wage	Post Secondary Education Or Training	Number of Children
John	LD	23	2000	No	Full time	$10.00	None	0
Tim	LD	23	2000	No	Part time	$10.00	None	0
Jack	LD	22	2001	No	Unemployed	—	None	0
Angie	LD	23	2002	No	Full time	$10.00	None	1
Lance	LD	23	2001	Yes	Full time	$10.00	None	0
Dan	Autistic	20	2003	Yes	Part time	$6.10	None	0
Janie	LD	22	2002	Yes	Unemployed	—	None	1
Sam	LD	23	2001	No	Unemployed	—	None	0
Steve	LD	23	2001	No	Unemployed	—	None	0

Figure 6.1. Demographics of the Graduates

John was a clean cut, 23-year-old young man with dark brown hair. He had graduated from high school in May 2000. John was classified as having a learning disability when he was in school. Initially in school he needed special education classes in reading, written language, and math. By his senior year he was only in special education classes for math.

John began working as a dishwasher at a restaurant about 15 miles from his house while he was still in high school. He also received his driver's license while he was in high school. He drove to his job and earned high school credit for working. He worked his way up to a cook at the restaurant and within five years became a kitchen manager earning $10.00 an hour.

John did not enjoy his work. He really wanted to be a writer when he was in high school. In order to help him achieve his goal, he took basic language arts classes in high school. John did not go on to college because he did not have the money to do so.

He also had the dream of being a personal trainer. He had participated in body building for approximately four years, and he had won many competitions. He hadn't really investigated where or how he could receive training to be a certified personal trainer. He did talk to a personal trainer at a gym who said he became certified through an Internet site, but John said he would rather get his training at a place where he could participate in class.

The reason John wanted to attend class in person rather than via the Internet was because of his disability. He believed he could receive more personalized instruction in a classroom setting. He did not believe he would be successful enrolled in an online program.

During his free time he could always be found at the gym. John's dream of being a personal trainer was a realistic goal; it was simply a matter of connecting with someone or an organization where he could get formal training and certification.

Tim

Tim was a 23-year-old man. He was very pleasant and polite. Tim was identified with a learning disability early on in school, and throughout all of his years in school he received special services in the special education classroom for reading, written language, and math. He graduated from high school in May of 2000. Tim lived at home with his parents.

Tim's mother remembered that his goal in high school was to graduate and work as a mechanic. He was fortunate in high school, because he was released early to go to a local mechanic's shop to work every day during his junior and senior year, but he was unable to achieve his goal after graduating. He did however utilize the skills learned in mechanics to work on his own truck.

Tim had worked for the school district right after graduating from high school as a substitute custodian. Tim explained that in high school he volunteered to work with the custodian, and after graduation the school district offered him a job as a substitute custodian. He only worked in the position for about a year.

Tim had been helping a friend on various carpentry jobs. He worked part-time and was paid $10.00 an hour. He said that he was waiting to go to California to work as a carpenter with his friend and they were supposed to be leaving in a couple of months.

Tim also had his own business and proudly presented his business card. He was available for yard work and for hauling. Tim was buying his own truck, a 2001 Chevy. He had a driver's license that he obtained when he was in high school.

Jack

Jack was a 22-year-old man who graduated from high school in 2001. During school he was identified as having a learning disability and was diagnosed with an attention deficit disorder. The academic area he struggled in was math. When he was in high school he was in the general education classroom all day with accommodations and modifications.

When he was younger he took Ritalin for a while. As he got older, he did not seem to respond as well to the medication, so his mother took him off the medication and gave him an herbal supplement which seemed to be more helpful.

Jack had a pleasant and very polite personality and spoke with confidence. Jack lived with his girlfriend at her parent's house.

Karen and Greg were Jack's parents. Karen was a cosmetologist, and Greg was a Baptist minister. They expressed the frustration they experienced when raising a child with disabilities. They also expressed some satisfaction regarding the school system.

Jack wanted to be an actor since he was in sixth grade and that goal had not changed. He took drama in high school to prepare him for his goal. His high school drama teacher wrote a letter of recommendation for him when he applied to a school for acting, but he was denied acceptance into the school.

When Jack graduated from high school he spent the summer working at a theme park. He enlisted in the U.S. Navy by fall. When Jack was asked what motivated him to join the navy, he stated that the reason was twofold. The decisive factor was that he would earn the GI Bill to pay for college once he got out of the military. But it was his story about what attracted him to the military in the first place that was most interesting.

He was in a high school class watching the local television channel that all students watched during first period and a navy commercial came on; it looked exciting to him. The commercial had jets landing on the aircraft carrier and satellite technology and there was GOD Smack playing, which was a hard rock band.

It was the creative, upbeat, and youth-oriented commercial that caught his attention and pulled him in. The commercial did what it was designed to do and motivated the young man to enlist in the navy.

Since leaving the navy, Jack had worked several jobs. He had worked as a bouncer at a night club, a record retailer, and at the time of the interview he was working construction for his girlfriend's mother in exchange for room and board.

Angie

Angie was a 23-year-old woman who was diagnosed with a learning disability when she was in school. She graduated from school in 2002. Her area of disability was in math. She was in all general education classes, but received special support in math.

She was polite, friendly, self-confident, intelligent, and full of self-determination. She had an eight-month-old baby whom she supported financially by working full-time. The baby's father (her boyfriend) was not participating in the financial responsibilities of raising their baby.

Patty, Angie's mother, was in her late thirties. Patty had endured many hardships involving her relationship with her husband while Angie was in school. Because Patty was experiencing so many personal difficulties at home while Angie was in school, she was unable to recall much about Angie's education.

Patty claimed that her husband was verbally abusive to both her and Angie, and that was the reason Angie moved away. Angie lived with her boyfriend and his mother.

Angie spoke with confidence and direction. She had obviously been through a great number of difficulties, but managed to develop self-preservation skills to take care of herself and her child. She had goals and direction in her life. Her main concern in life was to provide for herself and her child.

Angie was involved in a nursing program when she was in high school. She felt it was a rewarding experience where she learned a great deal. Although it was an excellent vocational experience for Angie, she did not want to work in the medical field. She felt that the hours would be too rigid for her, and it would be too difficult for her to work, go to school, and take care of her daughter.

Angie was working as a veterinary technician during her fifth year after graduating from high school. This was her second job as a veterinarian technician in two different states. She expressed her feelings about her job, saying that she loved her job and loved animals. She said that her difficulties in math did not affect her progress in the jobs she held. Before her current job, she had been in retail, a waitress, and had her own pet sitting business.

Angie would prefer to make more money in order to better support herself and her child. She believed that becoming an interior decorator would be something that she would enjoy and would also increase her income.

She wanted to take online classes to achieve her goal. Unfortunately, Angie believed that she was unable to accomplish her goal due to financial challenges. Angie needed the money to buy a computer and purchase Internet services at her house. She was aware that she would probably qualify for financial aid, but felt that she needed the equipment before applying to the school.

Lance

Joe and Sandy were Lance's parents. Joe believed that Lance had difficulty in school because he had so many absences due to Lance's brother being sick with leukemia. As a result, Lance missed a great deal of school and had a difficult time catching up.

Lance was identified as having a learning disability in the second grade. His mother said that he had a difficult time with reading, and got behind in math when school professionals pulled him out of the general education classroom during math instruction to help him with reading. This decision resulted in difficulties in both reading and math.

Lance was a 23-year-old man who lived alone in a town approximately 40 miles from where his parents lived. He graduated from high school in May of 2001. He confirmed that he had difficulty in reading and received special help in reading and written language through basic general education classes that were provided by the school.

Lance wanted to be a mechanic when he graduated from high school, and he did get a job working in mechanics soon after he graduated, but could not make enough money, so he quit the job in mechanics and went into construction. He was employed full-time as a construction laborer and earned $10.00 an hour. He had been working with the same company for almost four years. He said he enjoyed his job, but needed to earn more money.

Dan

Cindy, Dan's mother, was employed by the school district where her son, Dan, went to school. She was an athletic woman in her late thirties. She ran regularly and participated in marathons.

Dan was a tall 21-year-old man. He had difficulty with verbal communication and was diagnosed in school as being autistic with severe cognitive impairment. Dan graduated from high school in 2003. Dan had many of the typical autistic characteristics and did a great deal of pacing back and forth, as well as repeating verbal phrases.

He was able to communicate verbally, but it was limited. His personality was pleasant, and he strived to please and do well. Dan did get frustrated at times and learned techniques over the years to handle the stress that life presented him. He was aware of his surroundings and the people in it and responded to them appropriately.

Dan worked part-time in supported employment at a local grocery store. Dan's mother expressed her satisfaction with Dan's job. Dan stocked the store's shelves with a person employed to assist him with his job.

This was a job he had while he was in high school and was part of his special education transition plan. Dan's high school transitional education also included classes in home economics (which provided him the opportunity to learn to cook for himself), money awareness, safety awareness, relationships, and sex education.

Dan was living in an apartment on his own, and his mother, Cindy, visited him twice a day to help him as he needed it. The first week Dan was living in his apartment Cindy helped him transition by spending the entire week with him. She went over to Dan's apartment each morning to make sure he was ready for his day program; a transportation company picked him up to take him to his program and bring him home.

Cindy went over in the evenings to help him with dinner and anything else he might need. This was a new experience for both of them because this arrangement had only been in place a few months at the time of the interview.

Janie

Janie was diagnosed with a learning disability when she was in school. She was a 22-year-old woman who graduated from high school in May of 2002.

Lori, Janie's mother, felt that Janie had been through too much emotional trauma by being identified as a special education student, and the stigma of being labeled and tormented by other students had caused permanent damage to Janie's self-esteem, affecting her life into adulthood. Lori explained that she just wanted Janie to forget about what she had been through.

Lori gave birth to Janie when Lori was only 15 years old. Lori said that during Janie's educational years she was concerned mostly with simply providing the basics for her daughter, such as food, shelter, and clothing. Janie was an only child. Lori was still living with Janie's biological father, although they were not married.

Lori often referred to her daughter as being slow, yet a very smart young lady, and a wonderful mother. Janie had a 10-month-old baby and was married to what Lori described as a terrific husband, and they lived as an independent family.

Sam and Steve

Ruth was a mother of twin sons, Sam and Steve, and she was very discouraged with the education her sons received. She felt that the stigma of special education did a great deal of damage to her sons' self-image.

Both of the twins were living at home. They were two men who were 23-years-old, and Ruth reported that they were not focused on anything in life. They were unemployed and receiving Supplemental Security Income. They graduated from high school in May of 2001.

Ruth believed that her sons wasted their time in school. They were identified as students with learning disabilities. According to Ruth, they spent a great deal of their time in special education classes with little or no academic expectations and never learned how to read.

TYPES OF EMPLOYMENT

Of the nine graduates, five of the nine were employed at least part-time. Three of them were employed full-time. The types of employment at the time of the interviews were mostly service jobs.

The jobs included construction laborer, kitchen manager, stock person for a grocery store, and veterinary technician. Other jobs they had acquired over the years since graduation were also service jobs including waitress, dish washer, pet sitter, custodian, maid, bartender, bouncer, and retail sales person. One student had been in the U.S. Navy for three years.

Obtaining Employment

Obtaining employment is usually a great challenge for students with disabilities. Students with disabilities are less likely to be employed after graduation than their peers without disabilities. It may also be difficult for some students with disabilities to maintain employment.

If the student is fortunate enough to obtain employment and maintain it, then they have to deal with the fact that the job most likely does not provide a livable wage. The jobs students with disabilities obtain are usually in the area of public service. The concern is that these jobs are often dead-end jobs with little opportunity for promotion.

Many do not find personal satisfaction in their jobs. They are often at a loss at how to go about gaining better employment. Overall, however, if the youth is able to obtain a job, then they make wages comparable to noncollege youth of similar age in the general population.

Both Jack and Angie always had jobs available to them and believed that if they wanted one bad enough they could always get one. This was not the case for the twins, Steve and Sam, nor for Janie. They were unemployed, and their parents stated that their lack of self-esteem and lack of motivation prevented them from even trying in most cases.

Janie did not have a driver's license, and her mother credited this to her lack of confidence. Steve and Sam could not read or write well enough to complete an application on their own.

It is typically more difficult for youth with disabilities to obtain employment, but this was not the perception of the students interviewed who were actively employed. However, for the four students who were unemployed, this was the perception.

The graduates all had a general idea that they would prefer having a job that they would enjoy and one that would provide a higher income. Except for Dan's parents (due to the severity of Dan's disability), the parents and/or guardians wanted to see their children go on to receive more vocational training after high school, and/or go on to a community college.

Jack was the only one who was confident that he could pay for continuing education, because he had the GI Bill available to him. Except for Jack, the graduates as well as their parents were at a loss on how to achieve the goal of secondary education or training, although their future goals depended on higher education and/or training.

Financial challenges are common among graduates with disabilities when trying to continue their education. Although their low income may qualify them for financial assistance to go to school, they do not always have the knowledge or guidance to follow through with the process of applying for assistance.

Wages

All of the graduates who were employed made $10.00 an hour, except for Dan who was making $6.10 an hour. They all (except Dan) desired an increase in wages. Statistics regarding wages indicates that people with disabilities usually make lower wages than those without disabilities. However, in the community where these graduates lived, their salary was commensurate with their nondisabled peers with similar education and work experience.

SERVICES THAT ARE NEEDED AND RECEIVED BY STUDENTS WITH DISABILITIES AFTER GRADUATION

Five of the graduates received state financial assistance after graduating from high school. Three were receiving Supplemental Security Income due to their disability. According to a report by the National Council on Disability and the Social Security Administration (2000), there is an increase of youths with disabilities who are receiving Social Security benefits and not leaving the benefit rolls.

Two of the students who were interviewed were receiving financial assistance from the state because they qualified as low income families. Both graduates who were also mothers were receiving Women Infant and Children services (WIC) for their children.

Angie's mother was able to help her connect with government assistance programs, as were Janie's and Dan's mothers. Parental participation in assisting students has been pivotal in their success.

If there was a coordinator available to assist these students after graduation with the paperwork involved in postsecondary education and training, then these graduates might be far more successful in continuing their education. The coordinator could also assist with the paperwork involved in obtaining adult services.

Independent Living

John really would have liked an apartment of his own, but could not quite afford one with the wages he was making. He worked hard and spent his money wisely, and he still was unable to live independently. This was the case with most of the graduates in the study.

Youth with disabilities are less likely to live independently than youth without disabilities after graduation from high school. It is common for youth with disabilities to continue to live with their parents or the parents of their significant other. They may also live with extended family, relatives, friends, or others as they transition into adult living.

Many of them do not have the skills or knowledge to access low income housing without the help of a service provider. Managing money and time, obtaining housing, and taking care of health needs are critical aspects of a student's education that can easily be overlooked. Government housing and assistance applications should be introduced to students while they are still in high school.

Youth with disabilities are less likely to achieve independent living than youth in the general population. Six of the nine graduates who were interviewed were living with family members or friends. Their financial status prevented them from living independently.

SUGGESTIONS FOR SPECIAL EDUCATION TEACHERS AND STAFF

Schools can survey their students with disabilities after graduation to get their perspective on the effectiveness of the special education program. The students and their parents can provide insight to the strengths and weaknesses of the program.

The surveys can be mailed out with self-addressed envelopes. Phone interviews are suggested for those participants who do not return the written surveys. This insight is invaluable for program maintenance and improvement.

SUMMARY

Many special education students, after graduating from high school, are unemployed or work only part-time. Their wages are not usually comparable with their nondisabled peers. Some students experience working in the community during high school as part of their special education transition plan and may continue with the same job or stay in the same field after graduation.

Most special education graduates do not continue on to post secondary education. Many of the graduates need to access Supplemental Security Income benefits, social services, and other types of assistance. Graduates need to be aware of what services are available to assist them before they leave high school.

Knowledge of adult services that are available to students after graduation is necessary during their transition period. Parental and/or other adult assistance in connecting with these services is of great help to graduates with disabilities.

Chapter 7

Quality of Life

"The most terrible poverty is loneliness and the feeling of being unloved. Let no one ever come to you without leaving better and happier."

Mother Teresa

INTRODUCTION

When evaluating how well graduates have transitioned into adult living, there is more to consider than employment. There are many factors to consider when evaluating a person's quality of life.

For instance, how do they spend their free time? Do they have friends? Are they involved with their family? Do they have risk-taking behaviors that affect their safety? Do they have any hobbies? Do they have positive self-esteem?

This type of information helps one to understand more about a person's life than whether they are simply employed and whether they are able to support themselves financially. It gives a fuller picture of their lives, because unfortunately, adults with disabilities often lead a life segregated from the general community. This chapter explores the experiences of special education graduates' quality of life, three to five years after graduation.

SELF-ESTEEM AND SELF-IMAGE

A new student in a special education resource classroom had only been in class for a few months. She was a reserved child who smiled a great deal and was always cooperative. One morning she was walking down the hall going to her special education class.

The teacher was standing at the door greeting the students as they walked in. As this young girl was about to enter the room, an older boy teased her about going into a special education classroom. The girl was devastated. She blushed with embarrassment. She smiled, trying to hide her humiliation, and looked down at the floor and darted into the special education classroom.

Poor self-esteem and poor self-image are common problems for students with disabilities. Positive self-esteem is necessary for optimal learning to take place. There is an abundance of stories of the haunting, teasing, and harassment that special education students endure from their peers. Students with disabilities have been identified by their peers as being slow simply by walking into a classroom.

Even if the classroom does not have a sign above the door identifying it as a special education classroom, the children in the school quickly identify the room for students with special needs. For many years, parents had to choose whether to allow their child to endure the possible stigma of being identified as a special education student in order to get the extra support their child needed, or to deny their child access to the special education support.

It is this aspect of the program that has done the most severe damage to the students in special education. This challenge may be one of the single most devastating challenges for students with disabilities to overcome and many continue to have poor self-esteem and self-image their entire lives.

Special education students may spend their lifetime hearing from their peers, teachers, and sometimes parents how slow they are, and hear discussion after discussion about their low academic achievement.

In most cases these students internalize this label and these comments and have labeled themselves as "stupid." For some students, the identification of needing special education began a long road of self-fulfilling prophecy. Low self-esteem can follow them into adulthood and negatively affect their success in transitioning into adult living.

Self-esteem and/or self-image is how the student perceives him or herself as a human being and his or her contributions as a member of society. It is a measure of value and self-worth.

Because first grade is when academics are usually introduced, many students with disabilities endure teasing and torment from fellow classmates from first grade on. Their self-esteem and self-image issues are confirmed by the fact that they are not being able to perform well academically and sometimes socially.

Therefore, it is important to identify the students' strengths and help them emphasize growth in those areas as well as remediate their weaknesses. Highlighting the student's strengths at the beginning of IEP meetings promotes positive self-esteem and self-image.

A student's program should be based on student interest as well. This approach can help increase attendance, self-esteem, and success. Developing and identifying other areas of achievement outside the academic area will also facilitate a healthy self-image.

Love and belonging is a basic human need. Maslow's hierarchy of needs is a theory that claims a human being must feel love and belonging in order to gain positive self-esteem. Positive self-esteem is needed in order for a human to obtain self-actualization, which is the ability to pursue inner talent, creativity, and fulfillment.

Drama and other fine arts programs have been known to have a positive influence on self-esteem. Performing arts classes can also give direction regarding career goals. Such domains as physical abilities, arts, and social skills are areas that most children can enjoy and develop in order to have a positive self-image.

Self-motivation and initiative are critical to students becoming independent, productive citizens. Learned helplessness can be a result of being overprotective of students with disabilities. It takes the right balance of maintaining high expectations and support. If the student's parents and teachers do not expect the student to succeed on his/her own, then it can result in the student becoming dependent on others.

Students with disabilities can experience realistic fears and imaginary fears which involve the perception of others. They may fear judgment by others and become self-conscious of their intelligence, abilities, and appearance.

PERCEPTION OF SELF-WORTH AND/OR SELF-ESTEEM

Janie

Janie spent all of her educational years in one school district. She was identified as learning disabled in first grade. She had a good experience in school until she reached middle school. In middle school she was singled out by the other students as being "stupid" because she was in special classes with students who were severely cognitively impaired. She began to believe that she *was* "stupid" and learned to hate school.

Her mother believed that the most helpful thing her education provided was job shadowing. She felt that the job at the veterinarian's office was a chance for her to get away from the class of "slow learners," but she also believed that the school should not have informed the veterinarian's office of her learning disability.

Janie's mother believed that the school district made a mistake by putting learning disabled students together in a special class with students who were severely cognitively impaired. She believed that this caused her daughter to hate school because her peers viewed her as "retarded", and she perceived herself as "retarded" as well.

Janie's mother believed that Janie's poor self-confidence stemmed from her being labeled a special education student, and that prevented her from achieving her goals as an adult. She believed that this was the reason that Janie had not taken her driver's license test and had not pursued higher education.

During the high school graduation ceremony Janie was assigned to walk with a severely cognitively disabled student because Janie was able to control the student. She did not even want to go to her own graduation because of this.

She was in charge of the student with severe cognitive delay all throughout her education because the severely disabled student liked her and behaved well with her. She was even assigned to sit with her at lunch and walk her to classes. According to Janie's mother, this was devastating to her social and emotional growth.

Lance

Lance's mother talked about how Lance was teased by his peers from an early age because he had to go to a separate classroom to get help for his reading disability. She felt that Lance may have gone on to higher education had he not internalized the belief that he was not smart enough. There were a few students in school that made his life miserable because he was in special education.

Angie

Sometimes the verbal and mental abuse may stem from the home environment. Angie's mother, Patty, felt that Angie's poor self-esteem had more to do with the verbal abuse from her stepfather. She said that Angie's stepfather would refer to Angie as "stupid."

Sam and Steve

A teacher told Ruth at a meeting that her sons, Sam and Steve, would never be able to learn much, and they would never learn to read. Ruth said that this was a declaration made to her and her sons with no regard to how it might affect them. Sam and Steve frequently referred to themselves as "dumb."

Tim

Joann, Tim's mother, stated that putting her son Tim with students who had severe cognitive disabilities was a huge mistake. She said that it slowed down the learning process for Tim and only reinforced the idea that he was "mentally retarded," when in fact he had a mild learning disability. Tim always felt "stupid" going into the resource room, and he was frequently teased.

John

John felt that his experience of being singled out as a special education student was a difficult one. It was hard on him being put into classes with students who were severely cognitively disabled. He did not believe that the school should put students with learning disabilities in a separate class with students with severe cognitive disabilities.

John believed that there should be lower student-teacher ratios. He felt embarrassed when he did not understand something during a lesson, so he did not ask questions when he did not understand. Like many students, he would rather get into trouble with discipline issues than be targeted by his peers as someone who was "dumb" or "stupid."

FREE TIME

The graduates expressed interest in spending their free time in many different positive and healthy activities. Most of the graduates interviewed in the study had hobbies that were personally rewarding for them; most of them enjoyed spending quality time with their family.

Having a disability does not necessarily put a student more at risk of using and/or abusing drugs and alcohol. However, Sam and Steve did have an addiction to drugs and alcohol, according to their mother.

Spirituality is not an area that school is equipped to address, but this is an area that can help make an adult life more enriched. Involvement in the community can assist in the spiritual enrichment for students.

Hobbies

The graduates had numerous hobbies they enjoyed. Janie belonged to a dart team and played regularly, but spent most of her free time with her baby. Angie went out with her friends, but spent most of her free time with her baby. Lance enjoyed riding dirt bikes and motorcycles.

John's hobbies were body building, writing, and playing Nintendo. Tim liked to go fishing and ride four-wheelers. He liked to make go-carts. He also had a hobby which grew into a business. He went around town and found free junk. He fixed it and then resold it.

Dan liked to camp and fish. He enjoyed going to the movies. He went places with his family and grandparents. He liked watching television and movies.

Jack spent his free time going out with his girlfriend and enjoyed playing the drums and guitar. He would have liked to make a career out of being a musician if his acting career was not successful.

SUGGESTIONS FOR SPECIAL EDUCATION TEACHERS AND STAFF

Teachers and staff have a tremendous impact on students. What a teacher or staff member says to a student and how they say it can make or break a student. They are sensitive to criticism and praise. What a teacher says to a student as well as how they treat the student may be one of the greatest influential factors of a student's educational success.

Teachers and staff must give students the same respect that a student is expected to give an adult. Public and/or private humiliation can do irreparable damage to a student's self-image. If the adults in the student's life emphasize the student's strengths, then the student and his or her peers will also. School districts should promote sensitivity training for all teachers, administrators and staff

SUMMARY

Students with disabilities have the same needs as students without disabilities regarding the need to have a well-balanced life. Employment is important to adult living, but socializing, hobbies, self-esteem, relationships, and having fun can help provide balance in their lives.

Hobbies can help children as well as adults occupy their time and enrich their lives, and help to avoid destructive behaviors.

Teachers need to be patient and understanding. If students with learning disabilities are pulled out of the general education classroom along with students who are severely cognitively impaired, it creates the risk of further stigmatization.

Too often, a student with a disability, and the teachers, parents, and peers around them see the disability first and do not recognize what the student is actually capable of. Therefore, this perception is internalized by the student and results in poor self-image.

Students' strengths should be emphasized even more than their weaknesses. Their strengths should be built on and expanded to help the student grow in self-confidence and self-worth. Students' strengths and interests should be identified and utilized as catalysts to improve on areas of weakness.

Chapter 8

Do Schools Prepare Special Education Graduates for Adult Living?

"Whatever you are, be a good one."

Abraham Lincoln

When special education students graduate from high school, they move into another stage in their lives as adults. This chapter presents the graduates' perspectives of how well schools prepared them for adult living. The parents of graduates provide a perspective which may or may not mirror that of their child's.

There is great value in understanding these different viewpoints. Such information gives educators insight into what is needed in order to develop new programs and improve on existing programs.

Expectations of students' daily living skills dealing with finances, rent, insurance, and other needs such as having a checking account, saving money, and filing for taxes are areas that need instruction during high school. Students need to understand the realistic financial situations they will face after graduation. Too often students graduate from high school without the basic knowledge of the financial responsibility it takes to live on their own.

Special education students need to develop basic academic skills to their highest possible potential. Basic math and reading skills are necessary for young adults to be able to apply for and keep jobs. They need these skills for both work and leisure.

Regular attendance and punctuality are essential job skills. Knowing how to get along with others and communicate effectively are also skills needed for job retention.

SUCCESS

How is success defined for students with disabilities? When reviewing the experiences of students with disabilities, success needs to be defined. Success for each person is something different.

What is the end goal for these students? Independent living is the goal for the majority of students with disabilities. However, for students with more severe disabilities, independent living is not in the realm of possibility.

For some students with emotional and behavioral disabilities, remaining alive and out of jail or prison is considered a successful transition.

Special education teachers, students, and parents all may have a different definition of success for the same child. Parents may have goals for their child that exceed everyone else's. For a young adult with a learning disability successful transition may be independent living with postsecondary education or training and a career or a good job.

Access to transportation and medical services would also be considered priority. A successful transition may include a driver's license and means of transportation as well as good mental and physical health. For a young adult with severe mental or cognitive impairment successful transition may be defined as semi-independent living with adult services in place and government assistance.

In the majority of cases are bare minimum standards for success met? Dare we go beyond just the basic elements of the above definitions of success? Can we prepare our students for more than shelter, food, and transportation?

Most of the students in the study were very successful. Many of them were employed and earning wages comparable to their nondisabled peers. They cited many aspects of their education which prepared them for successful transition into adult living. Most of the students in the study had a good quality of life with family and friends and hobbies they enjoyed.

Society may define success in terms of money and education. This study implies that there is more to success than one's earning potential. Happiness and a good quality of life are important factors in the formula of success.

HIGHLY QUALIFIED TEACHERS AND HIGH-QUALITY TEACHERS

Individual teachers who go the extra mile for their students are a significant factor in the growth and development of students with disabilities. Most people can recall a special teacher or teachers in their lives that made an impact on their future. These teachers take an individual interest in their students.

Students and parents recognize specific teachers as being a great influence in their lives. A high-quality teacher may be defined as one who goes above and beyond the average teacher regarding communication with parents, administration, students, and other teachers. These high-quality teachers may reach beyond the schools and into the community to obtain and coordinate community resources for the students.

Highly qualified, on the other hand, is a term used by a Federal Act, No Child Left Behind, to define the qualifications of teachers in order to teach certain subjects and grade levels. These teachers must take certain classes and pass certain exams. A highly qualified teacher may not necessarily be considered a high-quality teacher by students and parents.

The No Child Left Behind Act of 2001 (NCLB) mandated that schools raise the expectations for students and teachers. NCLB requires that all students meet all state standards by the year 2014, and this includes students with disabilities. The accomplishment of this goal is measured by high-stakes summative standardized tests.

Parents of students with disabilities may not be as concerned about the scores on standardized tests as they are about their child's performance in the classroom and learning in the content areas. Learning how to read, write, and do math, as well as learning job skills and job seeking skills are the areas where parents of students with disabilities are usually concerned.

Individual teachers may be the single most powerful influence on a student's education. The quality of the teacher and the respect, care, and attention they give their students stay with students for the rest of their lives. Consistently students with disabilities and their parents can give names of specific teachers who played a major role in their success while they were in school.

These teachers demonstrated a special interest in the students. They played an encouraging role in the educational process and transitioning of the students. Not everyone can agree on what qualities make a great or even good teacher.

Some may view a good teacher as one whose students perform well on standardized tests, while others may define a good teacher as one who is more focused on the social and emotional well-being of the students.

There are several attributes and characteristics which may identify a good teacher. The teacher should care enough for the student not to embarrass him or her when a student asks questions.

The teacher should take the time to explain and re-explain many times, using various instructional methods in order to help a student understand the curriculum. The teacher should be patient and willing to work endless hours on teaching skills that are difficult for the student to learn. The teacher should make the student feel as if they are capable and worthy of the time and attention that is needed to help them become successful.

STUDENT EXPECTATIONS

Raising expectations for students is a theme running throughout schools in the United States due to the federal mandate of No Child Left Behind. Schools all over the nation are providing professional development regarding how to raise expectations for students. It implies that simply raising the expectations will enable students to achieve them.

The missing piece of information is that there must be remediation and support for those students who do not have the academic ability to achieve at high levels. Students with disabilities need even more support and remediation than their nondisabled peers. To simply raise academic expectations without the support needed can cause more harm than good.

Expectations for students with disabilities may be lowered in an effort to help them succeed. Lowering expectations may also be a bias when it is automatically assumed how much they can or cannot learn. This is a dangerous mistake. Instead of lowering expectations, support should be in place in order to assist the students to achieve at the same level as their nondisabled peers (or as high as the student is capable of achieving).

Students do not always have the help they need from teachers to understand concepts they are expected to learn. As a consequence, they may be given assignments and tests that are too easy and not challenging or too difficult.

If lower expectations are implemented, then skill improvement is less likely to occur. Lack of remedial support and lowering expectations can be areas of weakness and a bias in special education programs. Unfortunately for some students with disabilities, the curriculum, instruction, and expectations may all be lowered.

It would benefit students if they believed that success was linked more to effort than ability. If students do not associate success with effort then they may lose motivation to put forth the effort needed to succeed. Effort and motivation are necessary for success in the workforce.

John

According to Grace, John's grandmother, John was always a quiet boy who kept to himself. When he was in school he didn't get into any trouble. Even though his parents had to travel because of their jobs, he always had his grandparents to take care of him.

Grace believed that John was in a bit of a rut. He worked out at the gym, went to work at his job at a restaurant, and had a truck that he paid for, including the vehicle insurance. He was in a rut because he was unable to further himself in a career that he desired.

Grace believed that his high school classes did not prepare him very well for adult living. She believed that the school could have taught him how to keep a checking account and how to write a check. She would have liked for him to have learned about making payments and paying taxes. These are all things she has had to teach him during his years after high school.

John felt that there were two things that prevented him from going on to college, lack of funds and his difficulty with math. He would have liked to have been taught in high school how to apply for financial assistance so that he could attend college, and to have improved his math skills.

On the other hand, John believed that there were some things that prepared him for adult living while he was in high school. John believed that the help he received in school from one particular teacher was one of the biggest reasons he was able to be successful in school.

It was because of this teacher's special interest in his success and those of his classmates that he continued to do his best. It was her belief in him and support for him that made the difference.

This teacher was significant because she cared and because she pushed John and her other students to succeed. She had high expectations and provided her students with the support needed. She listened to her students and never belittled them.

John found that the social aspect of high school helped him in his job. The ability to converse with others and work as a team helped him to be successful in his jobs.

John suggested that teachers need to have compassion and understanding toward students who are having difficulty in school. He suggested that although teaching can become routine, it was important for the teachers to individualize and differentiate their instruction. According to John, teachers should try to make their lessons interesting and applicable to real life.

Tim

Joann, Tim's mother, believed that Tim really benefited from the job internship program that Tim participated in. She felt he should have enrolled in more vocational classes. Tim's mother wanted to see more education for her son in the area of relationships with peers, colleagues, and with the opposite sex.

Joann believed that the school should have provided Tim with a class that covered information on having relationships with the opposite sex. She believed that there should have been more sex education on a level that her son could understand.

Joann also felt that Tim should have been challenged more in school. Joann believed that the school should not have modified tests without allowing him the opportunity to take the tests without modifications first. She believed that the school lowered the expectations too much for him.

Jack

Jack was diagnosed with Attention Deficit Hyperactivity Disorder (ADHD) at the end of his first grade year. When he was in special education he had a one-on-one adult with him at all times until his fourth-grade year. In the middle of his fourth-grade year he was mainstreamed (included in the general education classroom) for the afternoon. In his fifth-grade year he was mainstreamed full-time.

By the second semester of fifth grade Jack was on Ritalin (a medication for ADHD). He was positive and enthusiastic, but he could not stay on task. He rarely handed in any of his assignments, and he never brought a book home.

Karen, Jack's mother, expressed her concern that the schools promoted Jack on to the next grade when he should have been retained. She perceived that the school system would have better prepared Jack for adult life had he been retained in the appropriate grades until he learned what he needed to learn before being promoted to the next grade.

On the other hand, she knew that Jack was a physically large boy, and he would have been physically out of place had he been retained. Karen recalled her son failing an entire year, and he was still promoted to the next grade. Greg, Jack's father, went on to express the frustration that they felt in regards to Jack, and his lack of preparedness for high school, and lack of preparedness for adult living.

In contrast to his parents' perception, Jack perceived his education as preparing him well for transitioning into adult living. Attendance, turning in assignments on time, being on time, and earning grades were some of the requirements that Jack identified as helping him most in life. He believed that those basic requirements help to develop a person's character and promote success.

Lance

Lance felt that the Home Economics class prepared him the most for adult living. Both Lance and his father believed that Lance would have been better prepared for adult living had Lance been able to enroll in more vocational classes.

Lance's father, Joe, thought that secondary schools should put more emphasis on mechanics, woodshop, welding, and other vocational classes, since many disabled students are more mechanically inclined than they are academically inclined. Joe believed that there was not enough emphasis on what would make a person qualified to work jobs that disabled students would likely obtain.

Dan

Dan was a student with autism and a cognitive impairment. When Dan was in elementary school, Dan spent about 50 percent of his time in the general education program. Dan was only in the special education classroom for language arts and math instruction. Most of his life skills like personal hygiene, cooking, and cleaning were taught at home. Dan was taught about personal relationships at home by his mother, with some support in the general health class at school.

Although Dan was not at the mental age to be in a sexual relationship, his body was mature, and his mother had to address issues regarding sex and relationships. The school provided very little sex education for Dan that he could understand; therefore, his mother made certain that she addressed this area of human development with him.

Cindy, Dan's mother, explained that because of Dan's severe disability, they had to hold many meetings with the general classroom teachers, and as long as they did this before the teachers received Dan in their class, the school year would go much smoother.

Cindy identified the most helpful thing for her son in helping him transition into adulthood was Dan participating in the general education classes. In the general education classroom Dan learned how to socialize and interact with nondisabled peers.

SUGGESTIONS FOR SPECIAL EDUCATION TEACHERS AND STAFF

As good teaching practices impact students positively, the opposite is also true. One casual negative remark has been known to devastate a child's self-image and motivation permanently. Therefore, teachers should choose their words and actions carefully.

It cannot be stressed enough that teachers must maintain high expectations for students with disabilities. Far too often expectations are lowered by both teachers and parents once students are identified as having a disability. Low expectations are a disservice to students with disabilities.

There is a false impression that achieving a high grade in a class with low expectations improves a student's self-esteem and self-image. When expectations are too low it only communicates to the student that he or she is not capable of achieving what is expected.

Instead of lowering expectations, there should be support in place to remediate and facilitate success. Accommodations and modifications may be necessary for students to be successful in class, as well as extra support and varied methods of instruction. An average grade that takes effort to earn has a more positive effect on a student's self-image than a high grade where little effort is exerted and/or little or nothing is learned.

SUMMARY

Individual teachers, job shadowing and internships, general education classes, vocational classes such as Home Economics, Metal Shop, Health and Drama, and integration into general education classes all help students with disabilities transition into adult living. Special education classes help students who need remediation in reading, writing, and math, all skills that students need to transition into adult living.

Overall, the parents and/or guardians in the study perceived the students as needing to be better prepared for adulthood. They gave recommendations for the school to consider regarding better preparation for transitioning into adult living. The parents suggested that the schools provide a better education regarding relationships and sex education as well as other classes to help with developing life skills.

The students and parents agreed that schools should do the following: (1) have more vocational classes available for students with disabilities to take in high school, (2) raise expectations for students with disabilities, but in addition to raising the expectations, they need to (3) provide additional support for the students to succeed.

The students identified several aspects of their educational program which they perceived helpful in preparing them for transitioning into adult living. These aspects ranged from the everyday expectations such as attendance and following rules, to vocational classes, and individual assistance. Many of the students, parents, and/or guardians cited specific teachers as those who made the most impact on their educational success.

Success should be defined individually. Each person has different potential and desires.

A person's success should not be measured by society's expectations. Each individual must define his or her own success.

Chapter 9

Building Successful High School Transition Programs for Students with Disabilities

"The function of education is to teach one to think intensively and to think critically... Intelligence plus character – that is the goal of true education."

Martin Luther King Jr.

There are many aspects involved in building successful transition programs for students with disabilities. There should be an array of special education delivery models to address the academic, behavioral, and transition needs of all students with disabilities.

Independent living skills can be addressed through life skills classes and accessing community resources. Vocational programs are necessary for successful transition. Vocational programs include vocational classes and job skills.

COMMUNITY RESOURCES

Some students with disabilities may qualify for Supplemental Security Income or other government assistance. WIC (Women Infant Children) is a program that can help young mothers provide good nutrition for their children.

There should be a class that includes learning about low income housing requirements. In some states there are certain requirements besides being in a low income bracket to qualify for housing. While they are still in high school students need to learn the requirements in qualifying for low income housing, as well as the application process.

Some of the problems people have in qualifying for low income housing are bad credit and poor references. If an applicant has poor credit, especially regarding utilities, and/or if their previous housing references are poor, then the applicant may be disqualified for low income housing.

A basic level of consumer finance should be in place for students with disabilities. Vocational rehabilitation can help students get into training programs and/or other post secondary education. Food stamps and cash assistance as well as mental health and medical assistance are all community resources which may need to be accessed by graduates with disabilities.

There is a process of applying and reapplying periodically for these benefits and services. Many recipients lose their benefits because they fail to follow the guidelines that are required to continue to receive benefits. The guidelines and requirements for the variety of state and federal programs should be taught while students are still in high school.

DEVELOPING VOCATIONAL CLASSES

Vocational classes, job shadowing, and/or internships are programs that have a huge impact on successful job obtainment for graduates. Students who received credit for working in the community at various businesses may receive high school credit.

This provides students with job experience and job connections for their future as well as earned credit toward graduation. It also gives the businesses opportunity to work with the students and open doors for both businesses and students.

A partnership between the high school, community colleges, and community businesses can be highly effective. Nursing programs, welding and woodshop, the arts, and job shadowing are all components of a vocational program which helps students develop skills and interest in careers after graduation.

More work-based learning opportunities tied to vocational programs are recommended for high schools. Finding the resources to provide the work experience or internships present a challenge. Therefore, it is critical to work in collaboration with the community and local businesses.

Vocational programs, especially those types of programs that require hands on learning, will help keep students in school as well as prepare them for work after high school. Placement on job sites is recommended for school credit. High schools and community colleges can form a partnership for students to receive dual credit.

Vocational programs contribute to keeping students interested in school, because they provide kinesthetic learning, which is an important learning style for students with disabilities. The students are inspired to work and become less threatened about the possibility of becoming employed. The students who participate in job shadowing or internships and vocational classes have an increase in employment opportunities.

Developing vocational programs can be difficult for school districts due to the financial burden on schools. There are many stages involved in developing vocational classes. The district or in some cases cooperating districts should first form a committee to discuss and plan for the logistics of developing the class or classes. Communication with the state department of education should be implemented when planning to add vocational classes.

The committee will need to determine which vocational classes are needed. Students can be surveyed to determine interests. Student interest, as well as community, region, state, and national economical resources may drive which classes are offered. The careers and/or jobs that are in demand regionally or nationally may be a driving force for development of vocational classes and/ or programs.

The committee must determine the resources necessary to pay for the instructor, the facility, and equipment. The district(s) may decide to partnership with businesses, colleges, and/or agencies in the community to fund and provide various resources such as an instructor, facility, and equipment for the class or classes.

There should be an advisory committee to oversee the class or program. This team, once the resources and funding sources are secured, will be in charge of the development of the class and/or program. The qualified and certified instructor must be selected. The curriculum must be developed and aligned with vocational standards. The student enrollment should be selected and the quality of the program monitored. See figure 9.1.

JOB SHADOWING AND JOB INTERNSHIPS

Job shadowing is when students go into the community and work. The work may be volunteer or paid. It is usually part-time employment and supervised or simply monitored by the school district. This activity allows students to discover job responsibilities and explore various careers. The ultimate challenge is matching skills of employees (students) with skills needed by employers.

There are child labor laws that school districts and businesses must follow when placing students in job experiences. It is essential to be aware of these

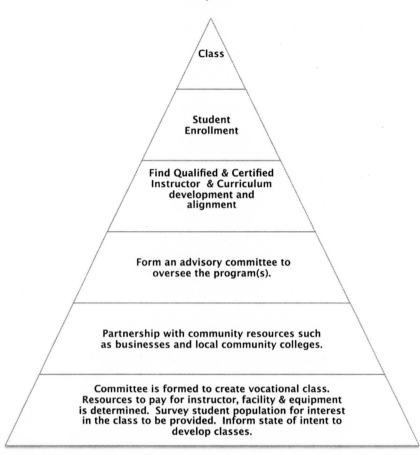

Figure 9.1.   Development of Vocational Classes

laws and ensure that these laws are followed. In addition, there must be safety training and orientation when a student is placed in a job experience.

Although job shadowing may temporarily slow down the productivity of the business, employers are often willing to make these sacrifices for the good of the students. The businesses are generous, but they must also consider their bottom line. Even in a training program some actual work must be accomplished.

Some schools require the student to find the business and/or job and then get permission from the school to obtain credit for working. Some school programs help the students find a job shadow host in an area of interest for them. That process can involve showing the students a database and letting them choose a host from the list. Often students are required to make the job shadow appointment themselves and provide their own transportation for the job shadow.

Another approach to this process is for the students to arrange their own job and get a training agreement from the coordinator. The agreement is signed by the student, parents, school, and business. The coordinator does weekly, monthly, or quarterly contacts with employers to evaluate the student progress and confirm continued employment. The student can receive academic credit for working a certain number of hours a week.

The coordinator also provides the students with job shadow paperwork that helps them evaluate the job and work site. After they make the job shadowing arrangements the student prearranges absence from school, which is excused as an activity absence.

Job shadowing and vocational internships require personnel to coordinate the outreach. If done properly the instructor can begin building a quality program, but it is easier said than done, especially in a smaller district with limited offerings.

Developing a school and community coalition can be beneficial to both the school district and the community. A district in Idaho has formed a coalition where community businesses, organizations, and agencies join with the school to help provide services to the students in the community's school district.

The superintendent works with the local newspaper to publish a monthly article to report on the various activities of the district as well as inform the public of the businesses who are in the coalition and how those businesses help the students in the community. All local businesses are welcome to join the coalition.

This type of partnership allows for a win-win situation. The businesses gain free advertisement through the publication of the articles submitted by the superintendent. When a business supports the district, a representative from the district writes an article about the business's contributions. Then the superintendent publishes the article in her monthly column in the local newspaper.

The businesses gain positive public relations as well as networking opportunities. In some cases the businesses are able to earn tax credit. The businesses ultimately gain the support of the community for their contribution to the children of the community. The community, businesses, and schools gain more responsible, social, and productive young citizens through this type of partnership.

The school district, in turn, receives support and resources from the businesses and community that enrich the education and social opportunities for their students. There are many areas where businesses and community members can supply the much-needed support and resources for the school district.

For many school districts the special education program demands a great deal of financial and professional resources to be effective. The special education program is one of the many programs where the school and community coalition can be supportive.

The school district can create a brochure to pass out to all of the local businesses where job shadowing and job training would benefit the students with disabilities. The flyer could include some or all of the following:

1. Information regarding the purpose of the partnership. For instance, "students with disabilities have a high rate of unemployment after graduating from high school. The school district is in partnership with the community to better prepare students for life after high school. The district is looking for businesses to join in the efforts to employ students in introductory positions while they are still in high school to develop vocational skills that will help students develop the skills that will make them successful employees."

2. Information regarding the type of positions the district needs for student placement. "Does your business have a position for a student employee? Introductory positions which require basic skills such as attendance and punctuality are needed for students. Does your business have tasks such as filing, cleaning, or stocking that need to be done? Does your business have a skill they can teach a student who is interested in a career requiring such a skill? Positions can be paid or volunteer."

3. Explain what type of disabilities students have and what businesses can expect. Students who need work experience may have a learning disability, which means they are having a difficult time with an academic area such as reading, writing, and/or math. These students may need extra support with learning certain skills.

   Other students may have a more severe disability which requires more attention. These students may have difficulty with socialization, cognitive functioning, and/or physical disabilities.

   Some students may have a physical disability requiring certain physical accommodations. Required accommodations will vary. For some students, adult support from the school may be required, while other students may not need the additional support.

4. Confidentiality. The district and the businesses must understand the confidentiality laws involved when working with students with disabilities. Written permission from parents must be obtained in order to release information regarding a student's disability, and the businesses must maintain confidentiality regarding the information they may receive.

5. Outline the benefits of hiring students with disabilities. There are many benefits to providing job experiences to students while they are still in

high school. When the students graduate they will have learned skills that the local businesses are requiring. The training provides a well-trained workforce available to the local businesses.

If the district is willing, they can provide free publicity by publicizing the partnership with the local community. The district can explain that they believe the community should be aware of the contributions of the local businesses. The businesses may also be able to receive tax credit by hiring people with disabilities.

The district can contact the state regarding any information that will financially benefit the businesses that hire people with disabilities and include it in the information they give the businesses.

6. Provide school district contact information for businesses if they are interested in pursuing the partnership.
7. Provide local contact information regarding the state child labor laws.

It is important for the district to follow up on the initial contacts made. Whoever is sent out into the community from the district should maintain a professional attitude and demeanor. They must remember that they represent the district and the students.

A FIFTH- YEAR COORDINATOR

A fifth-year coordinator for students with disabilities would serve as support for students transitioning from high school to the first year of adult living. This position would assist students with disabilities in completing applications, give job interest inventories, connect students with adult basic education resources, such as local community colleges, and help them locate assistance they need for supporting them with their disabilities.

The position could assist the students with disabilities in completing the necessary forms for applying for college and training, and completing forms for financial assistance and community resources. This position would establish a connection with the students during their senior year of high school, and continue throughout their first year after graduation.

SUGGESTIONS FOR SPECIAL EDUCATION
TEACHERS AND STAFF

All programs should use a student-centered process. A student-centered approach to education and transition means that the student's best interests are at the center of decision making. The student must attend the meetings and contribute to the planning. The student's parents must also participate in the planning, and both the student and parents must feel comfortable in participating in the process.

Teachers should use strengths, interests, and needs assessments to identify specific information for the student in order to provide a foundation for student-based planning. Finding the "best fit" between students with disabilities and employment is a productive form of planning for students with disabilities.

Not only must the student's strengths and weaknesses, along with their talents and interests be considered, but the employers and their tolerance for disabilities, are essential components of finding a good fit. Some employers are more tolerant and willing to train employees in areas where they need more assistance. Some job sites are more appropriate for students with specific types of disabilities.

Students with emotional disabilities, and/or attention deficit disabilities, hyperactivity, or behavioral disorders may be able to acquire the skills needed for a job, but they may lack the ability to maintain a job. These students may lack impulse control, and/or ability to deal with criticism and constructive feedback. Social skills need to be taught and practiced for all students, but especially students with emotional disabilities.

Students with emotional disabilities need a program which addresses problem solving situations, communication, impulse control, and anger management. A variety of situational circumstances and role play should be part of the program to prepare students for real-life social problems. Role play can help them plan and think ahead of time, teaching them how to react and prevent possible future problems with employers.

SUMMARY

Transition classes, programs, and activities are necessary for students with disabilities to receive appropriate transition services. This includes job shadowing, vocational and transition classes, and classes that teach life skills. Schools can collaborate with community businesses and resources to better serve students.

A fifth-year transition coordinator would be ideal for working with students one year after graduating from high school. Curriculum should include independent living, lessons to prepare students to connect with post secondary education and training, as well as adult services.

Chapter 10

Portfolio Development

Some school districts and even states are requiring special education programs to help students develop portfolios during their high school years as a tool to help them in their transition process. The portfolio can be an accumulation of materials and assessments collected over a period of four years in high school and kept in a three ring binder. Special education teachers and parents can facilitate the construction of the portfolios.

Portfolios can be used when applying for adult services and/or when applying for jobs as well as postsecondary education and/training. The portfolio contains highly confidential information and should be kept in a secure place under lock and key when being stored at school and at home.

The portfolio can be divided into many sections. The following are suggested sections.

1. Special education and personal records
   a) Most recent eligibility report
   b) Most recent IEP
   c) Medical reports related to the disability
   d) Copy of birth certificate
   e) Copy of Social Security card
   f) High school transcripts, diploma
2. Vocational assessment
   a) Course descriptions of classes that the student has taken which provide vocational and/or life skill training.
   b) Teacher interview/questionnaire
   c) Parent interview/questionnaire

  d) Student interview/questionnaire
  e) Volunteer experience in school, church, and/or community
  f) Paid work experience
  g) Computerized skills and interest assessments and inventories
  h) Achievement testing
  i) Independent living checklists
  j) Extracurricular activities
  k) Ability testing
3. Employment
  a) Basic resume
  b) Job applications for a variety of local jobs
  c) Cover letters
  d) Interviewing suggestions
  e) References
  f) Reference letters
  Employment agencies
4. Adult agencies
  a) List of local and regional adult agencies with phone numbers and
     addresses and contact names
  b) Pamphlets of adult agencies and their services and guidelines
  c) List of local, regional, and state adult agencies that have been invited
     to IEP meetings, including those agencies that are applicable to the
     student and his/her disability
  d) Applications for adult services completed by student and parent. If they
     have been submitted to the agency, then include a copy of the submit-
     ted form and date and location of when and where it was submitted.
     Blank applications are also useful for future use.
5. Postsecondary education and training
  a) Program requirements for degrees, certifications and programs from
     various local and regional colleges and trade schools of interest
  b) Tours of local colleges and vocational trade schools
  c) Name and phone number of advisor
  d) Name and phone number of disability service office
  e) Financial aid application
  f) Assistive Technology Assessment and Report
6. Independent living
  a) Inventory or checklist of self-care skills
  b) Housing availability and financial assistance applications
  c) Sample budgets as a reminder of the basic costs for survival costs
  d) Public transportation available locally, regionally, and statewide
  e) Does the student have a driver's license?

f) Does the student have a car?

g) Proof of insurance

SPECIAL EDUCATION AND PERSONAL RECORDS

Special education and personal records are important for students to gather and be able to locate when applying for adult services. The records may be needed for adult services such as Social Security, Vocational Rehabilitation, Medicaid, college disability services, Department of Developmental Disabilities, Health and Welfare services, and any other necessary services.

The types of personal and educational records that may be needed in the application process for various adult services may include the most recent eligibility report, the most recent IEP, medical reports related to the disability, a copy of his/her birth certificate, a copy of his/her Social Security card, and high school transcripts/diploma.

The difficulty with collecting this type of information and keeping it in a portfolio is the confidentiality of the documents. It is important that the portfolio is kept in a secure location not available to other students. Students should be made aware of the danger of such personal information getting into the hands of others.

VOCATIONAL ASSESSMENT

As indicated in previous chapters, it is a legal requirement for part of the transition planning to include a vocational assessment. A vocational assessment is an accumulation of data collected over time to assess the student's needs for vocational services.

The data that is collected can be stored in the portfolio for future use in deciding which jobs the student might be best suited for or which career path to follow. There are many computer programs that can help students investigate careers, colleges, and training options.

Course descriptions of classes that the student has taken which provide vocational and/or life skill training can be accessed from the high school course catalog. If a course catalog is not available, then perhaps the teachers have syllabi available. Interviews and questionnaires are used to get practical information that has been observed or experienced over the years.

Both volunteer and paid experiences are of equal value for determining jobs the student may enjoy and/or have interest in pursuing. The experiences will also provide an insight into the skills that are needed for employment.

There are computer programs that are available to help students access jobs that are available locally and nationwide. The computer programs may provide a salary and availability comparison. Some computer programs can also provide checklists, skills inventories, and interest assessments. Independent living checklists and assessments, both computerized and otherwise, provide a guide for the student and parents to assist in determining what type of housing and personal care assistance the student may need.

EMPLOYMENT

The section in the portfolio for employment will assist in the obtaining of various jobs. It can help in the systematic application for employment. The student should practice creating a basic resume and cover letter that he/she can include with job applications. The student can also use the resume to help them complete job applications.

It could be helpful to include resume guidelines and other sample resumes. The basic job resume could also be saved on a compact disc for students to put in the pocket of their portfolio binder. This allows for the student to amend the resume as they obtain more job experience and/or education/training.

The student can collect job applications from local businesses and get assistance and practice completing them. If the student completes and submits the application(s) then he/she can keep a copy of them in his/her portfolio in case they need to use the copies as a guide to complete new applications to be resubmitted at a later date. Students need to learn to complete professional-looking applications and resumes.

Names and contact information of references are handy to have in the portfolio. They can be from teachers, past employers, and supervisors where the student has volunteered. Reference letters are great to have for job applications as well as for entrance into educational programs.

Information from the local employment agencies can assist in helping the student obtain jobs. Many employment agencies have Web sites where students can surf job availability and salaries. There is usually an online application process as well.

ADULT AGENCIES

When a student leaves high school they may not have the financial and medical support previously provided to him/her. Adult agencies may or may not be appropriate for each individual student. Collecting information on what services the different agencies provide and the requirements needed to qualify for services can help the student determine whether they may be able to access the services.

The student and the parents should become familiar with the adult agencies and the services that are offered. If any of the agencies need to participate in the student's IEP, then it is the responsibility of the special education program to invite them.

A list of local, regional, and state adult agencies that have been invited to IEPs and those agencies that are applicable to the student and his/her disability can be a useful part of the portfolio as a reminder to the student and his/her parents of where to go and who to speak to for assistance.

Applications for the adult service agencies should be included to give the student a head start. Teachers and parents can both help the student complete these applications. Completing and submitting applications to the correct agency can be an overwhelming task and providing assistance in this area can be extremely helpful to the student.

Unfortunately, many youth with disabilities do not go on to attend post secondary education and training. Guidance in helping the student discover which schools offer the programs and training needed to meet the requirements for certain jobs and careers can significantly increase the odds that a student will attend postsecondary education and training programs.

Most schools offer a service to help with accommodations for students with disabilities. Accommodations such as giving the student additional time to complete assignments and tests can make the difference between a student dropping out or graduating. Students need to be aware of these services and how to access them before they decide whether or not to attend these schools.

Accommodations for high school can be different than those allowed for college or for postsecondary education/training. The student should be familiar with their own needed accommodations and check to see if those same or similar accommodations are allowed at the post secondary school they plan to attend.

Something as basic as whether a person can live independently or needs support should be determined before a student graduates. As indicated previously, most students with disabilities continue to be dependent three to five years after graduating from high school. This situation can continue to be a problem long into a person's life if there is not proper planning and support.

A realistic perception of the financial and self-care requirements must be taught starting at an early age. Transportation is a key to getting to and from work, adult services, and the grocery store. Even if a student is able to obtain a driver's license and a car, public transportation should still be explored.

POST SECONDARY EDUCATION AND TRAINING

High school is the time to begin making connections with post secondary institutions. Students need to determine what areas of occupation they are interested in exploring. Once they have identified areas of interest, then they need to locate post secondary programs that provide education and/or training for their areas of interest.

Depending on the community, there may be limited post secondary resources. Transition programs can provide formal and informal visits to local campuses. Teachers can also invite representatives from the schools to speak to the student at the high school.

INDEPENDENT LIVING

Where and how a student is going to live after graduation from high school is often an area overlooked by secondary educational programs. Independent living should be explored during the last two or three years of high school. Identification of whether the student has the skills or is capable of learning self-care skills should be a priority.

Helping students learn where housing is available and what requirements are necessary to obtain and keep housing is important to their independence. Survival skills such as budgeting and transportation must be learned, and it is often not taught at home, so transitional programs should implement the teaching of such skills.

SUGGESTIONS FOR SPECIAL EDUCATION
TEACHERS AND STAFF

In addition to creating a portfolio binder for the students, teachers should create a similar resource for themselves. Teachers should locate and collect the names of local, state, and national agencies and organizations as well as contact information and organize this information in a binder or filing system. The agencies and contact information that can help with the following areas should be collected.

1. Vocational rehabilitation
2. Postsecondary vocational schools and programs
3. Department of Health and Welfare
4. College and university disability support services

5. Department of Labor
6. Employment offices and Web sites
7. Student advocacy groups
8. School and community resources for transition
9. Independent living/adult services
10. Disability organizations
11. Other local, state, and national organizations

SUMMARY

Portfolios are simply notebook binders assembled by students with the guidance of teachers and parents. These portfolios can be used to help students explore occupations, postsecondary education, and training. They can be used to guide students through learning more about themselves and their strengths and weaknesses.

These portfolios can be taken to adult agencies to apply for services needed for adult living. They should contain information to assist in applying for adult services, jobs, and college and/or training programs.

These portfolios can also be used by special education teachers and IEP teams to complete the required transition documents on the IEP. As the student grows and develops throughout the years, then the information in the portfolio will change. These changes should be reflected in their IEPs. Appendix A contains activities and worksheets that can be added to the student portfolio binders.

Appendix A

Transition Portfolio

For Student Binders

(Transition Activities and Worksheets for Students)

The worksheets and activities in this section can be copied and distributed to students to complete and place in a three ring binder as part of their Transition Portfolio. The Portfolio Transition Binder should include the areas mentioned in chapter 10 as well as the following worksheets and activities. The students can add additional information in the binder as the teacher and/or student determines necessary.

JOB SHADOWING

Name of student _____

Date_____

Name of business _____

Name and phone number of contact person at the business _____

_____

Did you pick up an application? yes__ no___

Date you returned the completed application _____

Name of person you returned the application to _____

Position(s) available_____

Position(s) applied for _____

Did you receive a response (if so, what was the response)?

_____

_____

_____

_____

Attach a copy of the completed application to this form. You may need to resubmit your application at a later date.

PARENT IEP QUESTIONNAIRE

Student's name _____ Date _____

1. What are your child's strengths?

_____

_____

2. What areas would you like to see your child receive help in?

_____

_____

3. What is your child's favorite subject in school?

_____

_____

4. What is your child's least favorite subject in school?

_____

_____

5. How does your child learn best?

_____

_____

6. Does your child enjoy school?

_____

_____

7. What does he/she like best about school?

_____

_____

8. What does he/she like the least about school?

_____

_____

9. Does your child have friends at school and/or at home?

_____

_____

10. What type of extracurricular activities is your child involved in?

_____

_____

11. What activities would you like to see your child involved in?

_____

_____

12. Has your child been to the doctor within the last 12 months? _____ If so, please provide information that would be relevant to your child's education.

_____

_____

_____

PARENT TRANSITION QUESTIONNAIRE

Student's name _____ Date_____

1) What do you see as your child's strengths?

_____

_____

_____

Interests?_____

_____

2) What hobbies does your child have?

_____

_____

3) What occupations do you think match your child's interests and skills?

_____

_____

_____

4) Has your child voiced an interest in certain careers or jobs? If so, what?

_____

_____

5) What are your expectations for your child after high school graduation?

_____

_____

_____

_____

6) What plans do you have in place to support those expectations?

_____

_____

_____

_____

7) Where do you see your child living after graduation from high school?

_____

_____

_____

_____

8) How do you envision your child supporting him or herself after high school graduation?

_____

_____

_____

_____

_____

9) Does your child qualify for disability assistance after high school?

_____

_____

_____

POST SECONDARY TRAINING/EDUCATION

Name of student _____

Date _____

Name of organization of post secondary school _____

Switchboard phone number _____

Name of advisor _____

Phone number of advisor _____

Training programs and certification programs you are interested in:

1) _____

2) _____

3) _____

4) _____

What are the entrance requirements?

High school diploma_____

GED_____

Test scores (ACT, SAT)_____

Required high school classes _____

High school transcripts_____

What are the requirements for the training and certification programs you are interested in (see school or organization course catalog)?

Math _____

English _____

Science _____

Social studies _____

Electives_____

Major courses _____

_____

_____

_____

_____

_____

_____

Minor courses _____

_____

_____

_____

_____

Total number of classes or work experience/internship necessary to obtain certification or completion of program._____

How many years to complete program?_____

Will you work and take classes at the same time? _____

Does the institute have tutoring resources and/or services for the disabled?

_____

Name and contact information of the tutoring center and disability services office.

_____

_____

_____

Financial aid application due by _____

POST SECONDARY TRAINING/ EDUCATION CHECKLIST

_____ Contact with institute advisor

_____ Transcript evaluation

_____ Program and institution decision

_____ Contact with disability services

_____ Course of study

_____ Cost analysis

_____ Financial aid application

_____ Program calendar

_____ Class and internship schedule

COLLEGE PREP FORM

Name of student _____

Date _____

Name of college _____
Switchboard phone number _____
Name of college advisor _____
Phone number of college advisor _____

Degree and certification programs you are interested in:

1) _____

2) _____

3) _____

4) _____

What are the college entrance requirements?
High school diploma _____
GED _____
Test scores (ACT, SAT) _____
Required high school classes _____
High school transcripts _____
What are the requirements for the degree and certification programs you are interested in (see college course catalog)?
Math _____
English _____
Science _____
Social studies _____
Electives _____
Major courses _____
_____
_____
_____
_____

Minor courses _____

_____

_____

_____

_____

Total credits required for college degree or certification. _____

How many years to complete program? _____

Will you work and take classes at the same time?

_____

_____

Does the college have tutoring resources and/or services for the disabled?

_____

Name and contact information of the tutoring center and disability services office.

_____

_____

_____

Financial aid application due by _____

_____ Contact with college advisor

_____ Transcript evaluation

_____ Major declaration

_____ Contact with disability services

_____ Course of study

_____ Cost analysis

_____ Financial aid application

_____ College calendar

_____ Class schedule

INTEREST SURVEY

1. Which classes did you take in high school that you enjoyed?

2. What did you enjoy about the class?

3. Which classes did you take that you earned a grade of "C" or better?

4. What hobbies do you have?

5. What do you do in your free time?

6. What do you like to do?

Why?

7. What are you good at?

8. What do your parents do for a living?

9. What do your parents do for hobbies?

_____

_____

_____

10. Think of the people in your life what jobs do they do?

_____

_____

_____

_____

11. Are you interested in learning more about these jobs?

_____

_____

12. Go to the state employment Web site and look at the jobs available and list those jobs.

_____

_____

_____

13. Are you interested in learning more about any of these jobs?

_____

TRANSPORTATION

It is important to learn the local transportation system. Whether a person lives in a small rural community or in a large city, transportation is important. In small rural communities, there may be buses or community transportation for the elderly and for the disabled. A person can contact the Health and Welfare Department to investigate what transportation is available and who qualifies for the transportation. In larger communities there is often city transportation. There may be taxis and city buses.

School special education programs can facilitate students' obtaining the transportation information. They can also take field trips using the city transportation. It is important that students learn how to do transfers from one bus to another to arrive at their desired destination. It is also important that students know how much it costs and the time it takes for them to utilize the public transportation system.

Transportation activities can include planning small trips between work and home as well as a trip from one town to another or even as far as planning a trip from one state to another. The first step to utilizing public transportation is to identify and locate the available transportation in the student's community. Then a student can decide where they would like to travel and how often. The student can contact the public transportation office and begin planning.

Getting a driver's license may be an obtainable goal for some students. Taking a field trip to the local driver's license office is a transition activity that should be obtainable for most programs. The teacher could use the driver's license manual as part of a functional reading curriculum.

TRANSPORTATION ACTIVITIES

1. What public transportation is available to you in your community?
   a. Is there a city bus system? If so, collect the bus schedules and maps. How much does it cost to ride the bus? _____
   b. Where is the nearest bus station to your house? _____
   c. Your school? _____
   d. Your place of potential employment? _____
   e. Do you have a taxi service? If so, what does it cost to take a taxi? _____

   f. Do you have a Greyhound bus station in your community?_____ If so, what is the address? _____

      If not, where is the closest Greyhound bus station? _____

      Is there a drop-off or pick-up location to get on and off the bus? _____

      What sources of transportation can you use to get to the station? _____

   g. Do you have a train station in your community? _____ If so, what is the address? _____

      If not, where is the closest train station? _____

      What sources of transportation can you use to get to the station? _____

   h. Do you have an airport in your community? _____ If so, what is the address? _____

      If not, where is the closest airport? _____

      What sources of transportation can you use to get to the airport? _____

   i. List other private and public transportation available in your community and the cost to use the transportation. _____
      _____

2. Plan a trip using public transportation within city limits.
   a. Which public transportation is available to you to travel from one place to another within the city limits?

   _____

   _____

   b. How much time and money does it take to travel from your community to another city?
   Bus: Time _____Cost _____
   Taxi: Time _____ Cost _____
   Other transportation _____ Time _____
   Cost _____

3. Plan a trip using public transportation from your community to another city. Which public transportation is available to you to travel from one city to another?

   _____

   _____

   a. Which public transportation is available to you to travel from one city to another?

   _____

   _____

   b. How much time and money does it take to travel from your community to another city?
   Bus: Time _____ Cost _____
   Taxi: Time _____ Cost _____
   Other transportation _____ Time_____
   Cost _____

4. Plan a trip using public transportation from your state to another state.
   a. Get a map and determine your destination. Where do you plan to go?

   _____

   b. What type of transportation will get you there (plane, train, bus)?

   _____

   _____

   c. Check the prices and length of travel time of the following types of transportation to get you from the state where you live to another state of your choosing.
   Travel by airplane–Location of airports
   a. Depart location _____ b. Arrival location _____
   Length of travel time _____
   Cost_____

Travel by train–Location of train stations
a. Depart location _____ b. Arrival location _____
Length of travel time _____
Cost _____
Travel by bus–Location of bus stations
a. Depart location _____ b. Arrival location _____
Length of travel time _____
Cost _____

RESUME

Think of the job you are applying for. What skills, education, and training are necessary for obtaining this job? Keep these in mind when writing your resume and highlight those areas on the resume. Each resume should be customized for each job application.

• Heading—Name and phone number and e-mail address

• Professional goal

• Personal and professional strengths

• Education

• Employment experience

• Volunteer experience

• Clubs, activities, organizations that you have participated in

• Classes that emphasize skills and training for the job you are applying

• Honors/awards

TRANSITION POWERPOINT

Students can create a PowerPoint to share with classmates and IEP team.

Slide 1:	Title Page:
	Name of student and occupation that the report is about
Slide 2:	Job description of the occupation
Slide 3:	Training and/or education needed for the occupation
	High school courses
	Volunteer work
	Postsecondary education/training: where are the programs located?
Slide 4:	What is the employment availability in the area? In the state? In the nation?
	What are the wages for this occupation?
Slide 5:	What is the student's plan to prepare for the occupation?

DISCUSSION REGARDING SOCIAL SITUATIONS IN THE WORKPLACE

There are many social and emotional that occur in the workplace. Those situations may evolve from coworkers, customers, clients, and/or supervisors. It is important to be prepared emotionally, socially, and behaviorally to deal with those situations appropriately. The following are topics for discussion and role play to be better prepared for difficult situations in the workplace.

1. Discuss what you should do if you are having a difficult time with a coworker?
2. What would you do if a supervisor asked you to do something and you did not understand the directions?
3. Role play with a classmate a discussion you would have with your supervisor if you had a concern about a difficult situation at work. Use one of the following topics to use for the role play:
   a) You believe that a coworker is stealing from the company.
   b) You need to ask for time off from work in order to go to a doctor's appointment.
   c) Your work schedule is conflicting with your school schedule.
   d) Your coworker is neglecting his/or her work and you are having to do the work for both you and your coworker in order to accomplish what needs to get done for the day.
   e) You feel you are being verbally harassed by a coworker.
4. You are having a difficult time getting all of your work completed in the allotted time period and you find yourself working longer hours than you are assigned in order to get your work done. What should you do?
5. Role play the following situation:
   a) You are a server at a restaurant and the customer complains that you got the order wrong. You are certain that you have served them what they ordered. Role play how the conversation should go in order to deal with the situation in a polite and productive manner.
   b) You work at a hotel as a desk clerk and a customer comes to the desk to complain that the bathroom was not cleaned well enough. What do you tell him or her? What could you do to address the problem?
   c) You work at a fast food restaurant and a customer is complaining that you shortchanged him or her. How do you handle this?
   d) You work as a receptionist at an office and a client who has been waiting a long time comes to you and complains that he or she has been waiting for half an hour and wants to know what is taking so long and wants you to do something about it. What do you say and do?

6. Your supervisor calls you into the office and tells you that he or she has noticed that you have been coming in late. He or she tells you that if this continues that you will be dismissed. What do you say to your supervisor? What do you do?

7. Your supervisor calls you into the office and tells you that you are not working fast enough. What do you say and what do you do?

HOUSING

After high school graduation you will need to decide where you are going to live. Some will continue to live with their family after graduation. Some will want to live with friends, and others will want to live on their own. There are many different possibilities to consider when deciding where you will live after high school graduation. Answer the following questions to explore various housing possibilities.

1. Will you be attending post secondary education or training? Does the school you will be attending have dormitories where you can live?
2. Do you have a job lined up for after high school graduation? If so, how much will you make? Explore the local newspapers in the area you plan to live. You can go online to view the classified ads, and/or you can call local real estate agencies that handle rentals. How much of your salary will be necessary to pay for you to live in an apartment by yourself or with roommates?

   How much will it cost to rent a house?
3. What are the qualifications for government housing assistance? Do you meet those qualifications? What paperwork do you need to complete to determine eligibility? List the name of the local agency where you will apply.
4. How much does it cost for monthly utilities for a one bedroom apartment? For a one bedroom house? For a two bedroom house and apartment?
5. What causes the cost for utilities to rise and fall? How can you conserve energy in your house in order to reduce the monthly cost of utilities?
6. Is there local government assistance to help you qualify for utility assistance? What does it take to qualify for assistance?
7. Look through the classifieds in the local newspaper and/or online and list the lowest rentals available and the most expensive. What are the differences between the cost of housing? Do houses cost more than apartments? What are the deposits required to get into most houses? Do you have pets? Are they allowed in the majority of housing?

Appendix A

COMMUNITY PARTICIPATION

1. Do you ever go to the local post office? If so, what services are available at the post office?

   _____

   _____

   _____

   a. How much does it cost to mail a letter? _____

   b. How much does it cost to mail a post card? _____

   c. What are the flat rates to mail certain items? _____

   d. What is priority mail?

   _____

   _____

   e. What is express mail?

   _____

   _____

   f. How often do you use the services at the post office?

   _____

   _____

2. Where is the closest movie theater?

   _____

   _____

   a. How much does it cost to go to the movies?

   _____

   b. How often do you go to the movies?

   _____

3. Where is the closest bowling alley? Public gym? Basketball courts?

   _____

   _____

4. List all of the community activities in your area that you are familiar with and how often you attend.

   _____

   _____

   _____

5. What activities would you like to participate in that you do not know where to find?

   _____

   _____

6. Who could help you find them?

   _____

   _____

7. What clubs and community organizations do you belong to?

_____

_____

8. Would you like to find out about more clubs and organizations? If so, contact the local Chamber of Commerce, and find any information they can give you regarding community activities, clubs, and organizations.

PRACTICAL LIVING

1. Do you know how to open a checking and savings account at a bank?

   _____

2. Do you know how to write a check? And balance a checkbook?

   _____

3. Do you know the difference between a debit card and a credit card? If so, what is the difference?

   _____

   _____

4. What is a credit score? What would be considered a good credit score?

   _____

   _____

5. How does a good or bad credit score effect your life?

   _____

   _____

   _____

   _____

   _____

   _____

6. What do you need to do in order to have a good credit score?

   _____

   _____

   _____

7. What are the adult agencies in your community and what services do they provide?

   _____

   _____

   _____

   _____

   _____

   _____

8. Where would you receive help if you did not have enough food to eat?

   _____

   _____

   _____

9. Where is the unemployment office in your community? Do they have a Web site?

   _____

   _____

   _____

10. Where is your nearest public library?

    _____

    _____

    a. Do you have a library card? _____

    b. Does your public library have magazines? _____

    c. Does your public library have videos you would enjoy watching?

    _____

    d. Does your public library have computers you can access?

    _____

    e. What other resources does your public library have available?

    _____

11. Where is your community Chamber of Commerce? What information and resources are available there?

    _____

    _____

    _____

    _____

KNOW YOUR RIGHTS

1. If you were driving and a police officer was following you with sirens on, what should you do?

_____

_____

_____

_____

2. What are your rights if you were arrested?

_____

_____

_____

_____

_____

3. If a police officer gives you a traffic ticket or another type of citation, what are your responsibilities and rights?

_____

_____

_____

4. What other questions do you have regarding your civil rights?

_____

_____

_____

5. Get online and look up the term civil rights. What did you find?

_____

_____

_____

_____

_____

EMERGENCY SITUATIONS

1. Who do you call and what you do if your house is on fire?

   _____

   _____

   _____

2. What do you do if you have a flat tire?

   _____

   _____

   _____

3. Who do you call if you see a crime committed? What are your responsibilities as a civilian?

   _____

   _____

   _____

4. What do you do if your car overheats when you are driving?

   _____

   _____

   _____

5. What do you do and where do you go if you have seriously injured yourself?

   _____

   _____

   _____

6. What do you do and who do you call if you see someone who is seriously
   injured?

   _____

   _____

   _____

References

Adults with learning disabilities. (n.d.). Retrieved November 7, 2005, from http://www.audiblox2000.com/learning_disabilities/adults.htm

Blalock, G., & Patton J. R. (1996). "Transition and students with learning disabilities: Creating sound futures." *Journal of Learning Disabilities, 29*(1), 7–16.

Blueprint for Government Schools. (2005). *High expectations of all learners.* Retrieved November 18, 2005, from www.sofweb.vic.edu.au/blueprint/es/expectations.asp

Blumberg, R., & Ferguson, P. (n.d.). "On transition services for youth with disabilities." Retrieved November 7, 2005, from http://www.spannj.org/transition/transition_onpoint.htm

Bureau of Special Education Idaho State Department of Education. (2001). Idaho Special Education Manual.

Cameto, R., Camille, M., Mary W., & Cardoso, D. (2003, December). "Youth employment." National Center on Secondary Education and Transition, 2(2). Retrieved July 22, 2004. from http://www.ncset.org.

Carter, S. (2005). CADRE. "The impact of parent/family involvement on student outcomes: An annotated bibliography of research." Retrieved November 12, 2005, from http://www.directionservice.org/cardre

Creswell, J.W. (2002). "Educational research: Planning, conducting, and evaluating quantitative and qualitative research." Columbus, OH: Merrill Prentice Hall.

Creswell, J.W. (2003). "Research design: Qualitative, quantitative, and mixed methods approaches." Thousand Oaks, CA: Sage Publications.

Curtis, J. (2005). For families with special needs. Retrieved November 1, 2005. Http://www.childrensdisabilities.info/parening/snparenting.html.

Division of Persons with Disabilities Department of Human Rights. (n.d.). Strategic plan 2002-2005: Vision, mission, guiding principals. Retrieved November 7, 2005, from http://www.sate.ia.us/government/dhr/pd/images/html/StrategicPlanJune2003.htm

ESRC. (2004). "Life chances: The impact of family origins and early childhood experiences on adult outcomes." Retrieved November 12, 2005, from http://www .esrcsocietytoday.ac.uk/ESRCinfoCentre/PO/realeases/2004/june/lifechances

Garcia, C., (2005, June). Connect For Kids. *High expectations for secondary ed.* Retrieved on November 18, 2005, from http://www.connectforkids.org/ node/3205

"Gender as a factor in special education eligibility." *(*n.d.). Retrieved November 7, 2005, from http://www.iteachilearn.com/uh/meisgeier/statsgov20gender.htm

Global net. (n.d.). *Self-esteem enhancement: Self-esteem in education.* Retrieved November 10, 2005, from http://www.users.globalnet.co.uk/~ebdstudy/strategy/ esteem.htm

Gloeckler, L. & Dagget, W., (2005). "NCLB-A crossroads for special education." International Center for Leadership in Education.

Good, P. (2001). *In pursuit of happiness: Knowing what you want getting what you need.* Chapel Hill, NC. New View Publications.

Guilfoyle, K. (2005, September). Philosophical grounding of paradigms in research. Chart presented at University of Idaho class, Moscow, ID. Health Consultation. (n.d.). Bunker hill mining and metallurigical Kellogg, Shoshone county, Idaho. Retrieved November 11, 2005, from http://www.atsdr.cdc.gov/HAC/PHA/ bunkerhill91400/bun_p3.html

Hines, R.A., (2001, December). Inclusion in middle schools. ERIC Clearinghouse on Elementary and Early Childhood Education, Champaign, IL. Retrieved November 10, 2005, from http://www.ericigests.org/2002-3/inclusion.htm

Hocutt, A.M. (1996). "Effectiveness of special education: Is placement the critical factor?" (Electronic version). Special Education for Students With Disabilities, 6, no.1, 77–102.

Holmes, D.L., (2005). Advocate. "Autism: Navigating the turbulent road from adolescence to adulthood."

Horn W.F., & Tynan (2005). Time to make special education "special" again. Retrieved October 3, 2005.

Hughes, C. (2001). "Transition to adulthood: Supporting young adults to access social, employment, and civic pursuits." *Mental Retardation and Developmental Disabilities Research Reviews, 7,* 84–90.

Irizarry, D. (1999). The feelings of life. Grants Pass, OR: Grants Pass High Printing. Kellogg, Idaho Detailed Profile (n.d.). Retrieved November 11, 2005, from http:// www.city-data.com/city/Kellogg-Idaho.html

Kid Source. (2005). How do families learn to cope? Retrieved November 12, 2005, from http://www.kidsource.com/kidsource/content/learningdis.html

Kirsch, E. (2005, November 15). Shoshone News-Press. Kellogg, ID Kohler, P., & Field, S. (2003). "Transition-focused education: Foundation for the future." *The Journal of special education 37*(3), 174–183.

Kokko, K. & Pulkkinen, L. (2000). "Warm family environment protects aggressive children from school maladjustment and later adulthood unemployment" (Electronic version). *Developmental Psychology,* 36(4): 463–472.

Kunc, N. (1992). Axis Consultation and Training Ltd. "The need to belong: Rediscovering maslow's hierarchy of needs." Retrieved November 10, 2005, from http://www.normemma.com/armaslow.htm

Lincoln &.S., & Guba, E.G. (1985). Naturalistic inquiry. Newbury Park, CA: Sage Publications.

Loon, V.L, & Hove, G. V. (2001). "Emancipation and self-determination of people with learning disabilities and down-sizing institutional care." *Disability And Society, 16*(2). 233–254.

Love, L., & Malian, I. (1997). "What happens to students leaving secondary special education services in arizona?" *Remedial and Special Education, 18(5),* 261–273.

Marshall, C. & Rossman, G.B. (1999). *Designing qualitative research.* Thousand Oaks, CA: Sage Pub.

Martin, A. (2005). Living in my skin: Interview by Allison Martin. Retrieved November 1, 2005. http://www.childrensdisabilities.info/parenting/hickman-interview.html.

Martin, A. (2005). When your child has a disability. Retrieved November 1, 2005. http://www.childrensdisabilities.info/parenting/hickman-interview.html

Martin, E.W. & Martin, R., Terman, D. (1996). "The legislative and litigation history of special education" (Electronic version). Special Education for Students with Disabilities, 6, no. 1, 25–39.

Martin, J. (2004, October 6). Drama improves pupils' self-esteem, study find. *Guardian Unlimited.* Retrieved November 10, 2005, from http://education.guardian .co.uk/primaryeducation/story/0,11146,1320980,00.html

Martin, J. E., & Marshall, L. H. (1995). "Choicemaker: A comprehensive self-determination transition program." *Intervention in School and Clinic, 30*(3), 147–157.

McIntyre, T., Tong, V. (1998). "Where the boys are." (Electronic version). *Education and Treatment of Children,* 21(3), 321–332.

Mellard, D.F., & Lancaster, P. (2003). "Incorporating adult community services in students' transition planning." *Remedial and Special Education,* 24(6), 359–368.

Miller, Ross (2001, November). "Greater expectations to improve student learning." Association of American Colleges and Universities. Retrieved November 18, 2005, from www.greaterexpectations.org/briefing_papers/ImproveStudentLearning.html

Moran, C., (2003, February). Two-thirds of county students are males. Retrieved November 8, 2005, from http://www.signonsandiego.com/news/education/20030210-9999_1n10edkids.html

Murray, C. (2003). "Risk factors, protective factors, vulnerability, and resilience: A framework for understanding and supporting the adult transitions of youth with high-incidence disabilities." *Remedial and Special Education, 24(1),* 16–26.

National longitudinal transition study II. SRI International. (2003, February). *Sampling Plan SRI Project 3421.* Retrieved July 22, 2004 from http://www.ncset.org

National Center for Educational Statistics. (2000). Retrieved November 7, 2005, from http://www.cew.wisc.edu/followup/htm

National Center for Learning Disabilities. (n.d.). "A parent's guide to special education: Insider advice on how to navigate the system and help your child succeed."

Retrieved on November 10, 2005, from http://www.Ld.org/newsltr/1005newsletr/ 1005feature1.cfm

National Council on Disability: Social Security Administration. (November, 2000). "Transition and post-school outcomes for youth with disabilities: Closing the gaps to postsecondary education and employment." Retrieved November 7, 2005, from http://www.ncd.gov/newsroom/publications/2000/tranistion_11-01-00.htm

NICHCY News Digest. (1994). Children with disabilities: Understanding sibling issues. Retrieved November 12, 2005, from http://www.ldonline.org/ld_indepth/ family/family-sibl.html

North Central Regional Educational Laboratory. (2005). *High expectations.* Retrieved November 18, 2005, from www.ncrel.org/sdrs/areas/issues/educatrs/presrvc/ pe3lk24.htm

Parent Advocacy Coalition for Educational Rights. (n.d.). *Transition to the next steps after high school.* Retrieved November 7, 2005, from http://www.pacer.org/ legislation/idea/transitionNextSteps.htm

Ravitch, D. (1992, June). Kid Source. *Hard work and high expectations: Motivating students to learn.* Retrieved November 18, 2005, from www.kidsource.com/ kidsource/content3/work.expectations.k12.4.html

Sheldrake, S. & Stifelman, M., (2002). *The Science of the Total Environment. A case study of lead contamination cleanup effectiveness at bunker hill.* Retrieved November, 11, 2005, from www.elsevier.com/locate/scitotenv

Smith, S.L., (1994, summer). "How not to feel stupid when you know you're not: Self-esteem and learning disabilities." NALLD Center. Retrieved November 10, 2005, from http://www.nldline.com/self.htm

Soltman, M. & Pratt, B., (2005). Tough challenges, tough choices. Retrieved November 18, 2005, from www.sjisd.wednet.edu/sjisd/budget/Budget_Articles/ High_Expectations

Special Education Branch. (1986, August). "Special education monographs no. 3: Exceptional pupils with mild intellectual handicaps in secondary schools." Retrieved on November 10, 2005, from http://www.edu.gov.on.ca/eng/general/ elemsec/speced/monog3.html

State, County, and City Information. (n.d.). Retrieved November 11, 2005, from http://idaho.state-capitals.com/city/kellogg

Statistics Canada. (2005, January, 18). Study: Impact of family background on access to postsecondary education. Retrieved November 12, 2005, from http://www .statcan.ca/Daily/English/050118/d050118c.htm

U.S. Department of Education. History of the IDEA. Retrieved September 15, 2005, from http://www.ed.gov/policy/speced/leg/idea/history.html

U.S. Environmental Protection Agency. (n.d.). Superfund redevelopment program: Bunker hill finance case study. Retrieved November 11, 2005, from http://www .epa.gov/superfund/programs/recycle/success/financs/bunkhill.htm

Vaishnav, A., & Dedman, B., (2002, July). Bridges4kids: Building partnerships Between Families, Schools, and Communities. "Special ed gender gap still worry."

Retrieved November 8, 2005, from http://www.bridges4kids.org/articles/7-02/ BostonGlobe7-8-02.html

Wagner, M. Cadwallader, T. W., Garza, N. & Cameto, R. (2000, December). "Social activities of youth with disabilities." National Center on Secondary Education and Transition. Retrieved July 22, 2004. from http://www.ncset.org

Wikipedia. (n.d.). Kellogg Idaho. Retrieved November 11, 2005, from http:// en.wikipedia.org/wiki/UN/LOCODE:USKGI

Wolcott, H.F. (1994). *Transforming qualitative data: Description, analysis, and interpretation.* Thousand Oaks, CA: Sage Publications Inc.

Wood, S. J., & Cronin, M.E. (1999). "Students with emotional/behavioral disorders and transition planning: What the follow-up studies tell us." *Psychology in the Schools, 36*(4), 327–345.

Yelin, E., & Trupin, L. (2003, May). "Disability and the characteristics of employment." *Monthly Labor Review,* 20–31.

About the Author

Christy Mahanay-Castro has been working in the public school system for 25 years. She has worked in five different states and in a variety of positions including Director of Special Services, Special Education Teacher, General Education Teacher, and Building Principal.

She received her Doctorate of Philosophy in Education at the University of Idaho in 2006. She received her Masters of Education from Central Washington University in 1991 and a Bachelor of Science in education from Northern Arizona University in 1985. She has done graduate work at the University of Arizona and postdoctoral work at the University of Idaho in School Psychology and Counseling.

Breinigsville, PA USA
04 October 2010
246663BV00001B/5/P